PRAISE FOR THE HAPPY MIND

All of us want to be happy. *The Happy Mind* is a powerful roadmap for how to get there.
—MARIANNE WILLIAMSON, AUTHOR OF *A RETURN TO LOVE*

The Happy Mind helps us to become aware of the presence of love, which is our natural inheritance. And that awareness is the very essence of happiness. Dr. Yoder's seven principles remove our internal obstacles, and allow us to reclaim inner peace and joy.
—DR. GERALD JAMPOLSKY, AUTHOR OF *LOVE IS LETTING GO OF FEAR*

William Yoder has written a very important book that will be of immense help to countless readers.
—HUGH PRATHER, AUTHOR OF *MORNING NOTES: 365 MEDITATIONS TO WAKE YOU UP*

An insightful and easy-to-read happiness support system—Dr. Yoder empowers his readers to create a life of inner peace.
—BARRY NEIL KAUFMAN, AUTHOR OF *HAPPINESS IS A CHOICE*, AND CO-FOUNDER OF THE OPTION INSTITUTE & AUTISM TREATMENT CENTER OF AMERICA

According to the author, if we can hold in consciousness the non-dual reality of Love as Source until consciousness transcends duality, and if we engage in recommended practices, we will experience and sustain a quality of joy known as happiness. I recommend this book to all persons on a spiritual path.
—HARVILLE HENDRIX, PH.D. AUTHOR OF *COUPLES COMPANION: MEDITATIONS AND EXERCISES FOR GETTING THE LOVE YOU WANT*

Lucid, like a deep pool in which you can see right to the bottom: that is the way I would describe William Yoder's new book, *The Happy Mind*. No jargon, no cant, just a rare simplicity that offers a profound message to transform all living. This book will open doors that have been sealed shut for years and transform the reader's whole mode of being. It is not just to be recommended; it is a must.

—JAY G. WILLIAMS, PROFESSOR OF RELIGIOUS STUDIES, AUTHOR OF *THE PATH AND ITS POWER*, AND *THE SECRET SAYINGS OF YE SU*

We all have unconscious recipes for happiness that rarely bring us to our goal. To be happy regardless of your circumstance is the key to spirituality, wellness and relationships. William Yoder gets us beyond our mythology of happiness to help us find practical ways to experience and sustain it.

—DR. DONALD EPSTEIN, AUTHOR *12 STAGES OF HEALING*, AND *HEALING MYTHS HEALING MAGIC*

This is a page-turner! But not like a mystery is... Instead, an aura of peacefulness settles down with me whenever I read it... an odd, lovely feeling, especially these days. Bill's articulate wisdom has created a powerful system of finding "rightness with the world" and ourselves, and he makes it as clear as a meditation bell how to remember that this feeling is our natural state of being. My happy mind and heart are grateful to have received this precious bounty that was mine all along.

—PRUE BERRY, SERVED 27 YEARS AS EXECUTIVE DIRECTOR AND HOST OF U.U. ROWE CAMP AND CONFERENCE CENTER

It's the promise of the ages, a happy mind—and Dr. Yoder delivers on the promise. In these uplifting pages, he distills metaphysical insights and philosophical wisdom into seven practical, useful directives that real people can use in the real world and end up with 'happy' as their default mode.

—VICTORIA MORAN, AUTHOR OF *CREATING A CHARMED LIFE*

William R. Yoder, Ph.D., has written a delightful guide to *The Happy Mind* skillfully facilitating our movement into the moment when the choice for happiness is made. I appreciated his use of the basic principles of *A Course in Miracles* along with the teaching of the mystics.

—JON MUNDY, PH.D., AUTHOR AND EDITOR OF *MIRACLES* MAGAZINE

I loved the passionate way that Dr. Bill brought to the forefront how the mind works, and why we all deserve a "Happy Mind." In particular, on page 63, "One helpful way to think about this is that there is a *'place' in your mind*, a dimension of consciousness, a state of awareness where happiness is *always* available." Millions of people need to know this! Too many fall victim to the belief that while others may be happy, it's just not their fate. Dr. Bill explains quite beautifully that happiness is available for EVERYONE, and he shows us quite simply, how to get there. This book rocks!

—DAVID ESSEL, M.S., RADIO/TELEVISION HOST, AUTHOR
OF 5 BOOKS INCLUDING *SLOW DOWN: THE FASTEST WAY
TO GET EVERYTHING YOU WANT* (HAY HOUSE)

The Happy Mind delivers! Bill Yoder is on to something big in his thoughtful examination of our shared quest for happiness in life. Well grounded and practical, this book is eminently useful to those of us open to making happiness a choice. I wish I had read it years ago!

—THE REV DAVID S. BLANCHARD, UU CHURCH OF CANTON NY

Rather than write about his book, I would like to say a few words about Bill Yoder. Not only is he happy, but he is a very kind man and he is a healer. He gave up his prestigious college professorship to become a chiropractor … but he didn't abandon his philosophical quests. He applied them to a fundamental concern for people: how to be happy. Would that there were more philosopher-healers like Dr. Yoder.

—DOUGLAS WILSON, UNITARIAN UNIVERSALIST MINISTER
AND EXECUTIVE DIRECTOR OF ROWE CAMP
AND CONFERENCE CENTER

Happiness seems natural to children, but as we "grow up," we seem to lose this awareness and go on an endless search for this elusive gift. What happened to it? Where did it go? Nowhere. Happiness is our inheritance and needs only to be uncovered, not recreated. Through *The Happy Mind*, Bill Yoder offers us steps to uncover the gift of happiness that still abides within our hearts.

—BEVERLY HUTCHINSON McNEFF, FOUNDER OF MIRACLE DISTRIBUTION CENTER, WORLDWIDE CONTACT POINT FOR *A COURSE IN MIRACLES*

The Happy Mind is an excellent work that presents the basic universal truths in clear, simple and innovative ways. It will make a major difference in helping many to reclaim their birthright of love and happiness.

—CAROL HOWE, AUTHOR OF *NEVER FORGET TO LAUGH: PERSONAL RECOLLECTIONS OF BILL THETFORD, CO-SCRIBE OF A COURSE IN MIRACLES*

A NOTE TO MY READERS

Happiness is a state mind, rather than a state of affairs. Each of us is ultimately responsible for his or her own happiness. But this idea of responsibility is often misinterpreted. I am writing this note to avoid some of the most common misunderstandings.

1. Blame serves no purpose. Unhappiness or suffering is a *quality* of experience, rather than a matter of circumstances. Moreover, it is a quality that we ourselves add to our experience. But that does *not* mean that you are to blame for all of the difficult and challenging circumstances of your life. I don't know, for instance, why some people get cancer and others don't. But I do believe that we ourselves add the elements of fear and conflict and struggle to our experience of those circumstances.

This is not a damning accusation but rather the promise of hope, because it implies that we can liberate ourselves from suffering. And when we do, we reclaim happiness whether or not our circumstances change. So please do not misunderstand anything in this book as blaming you in any way. Blaming never helps the healing process. Blame only adds guilt and frustration to the suffering you're already experiencing.

2. You seek truth for more truth, not for more world. Or, as Hugh Prather remarked in an e-mail, "you should only seek God for more God. You should never seek God for more world (more health, wealth, etc.). The greatest hindrance to spiritual progress is the belief that there should be some reward in the world for our spiritual efforts." You can think of the spiritual journey as becoming aware of your truth as a being of love. And that awareness is the source of true happiness. But you cannot awaken to that truth while you are attached to getting something else.

3. The manifestation of your desires does not mean changing the world or getting stuff—it means happiness. Attachment to the world being a certain way is the underlying cause of unhappiness. This can take the form of either a positive attachment ("I need that new car in order to be happy"), or a negative attachment ("I need for my disease to go away in order to be happy").

Being happy is ultimately a matter of discovering the truth of joy within yourself, and is independent of worldly circumstances. When you are happy, you can still have your desires and pursue them with passion. But you are not desperately trying to change the world, thinking that something needs to be different for you to be happy. When you are happy now, you are *already* manifesting the deepest essence of *all* of your desires.

So welcome to *The Happy Mind.* I hope you enjoy this book and that it helps you on your journey to self-discovery and happiness. Some of the ideas may seem a little abstract in the beginning, but they will become very concrete and practical as you proceed. I strongly encourage you to read the chapters in order, since each one builds on the last. I would love to hear your comments and feedback. You can contact me through my website *www.TheHappyMindBook.com.*

THE HAPPY MIND

SEVEN
PRINCIPLES TO
CLEAR YOUR
HEAD AND LIFT
YOUR HEART

WILLIAM R. YODER, PH.D.

Alight Publications, New York

The Happy Mind
Seven Principles to Clear Your Head and Lift Your Heart
by William R. Yoder, Ph.D.

Published by
Alight Publications
Post Office Box 524
Sauquoit, New York 13456

Cataloging-in-Publication Data

Yoder, William R. (William Robert)
  The happy mind: seven principles to clear your head and
  lift your heart / William R. Yoder. — 1st ed.
    p. cm.
    LCCN 2010902553
    ISBN 978-0-9721556-1-8
    1. Happiness 2. Self-actualization I. Title.
BF575.Y63 2010

Printed in U.S.A. on acid-free paper

Author photo by NYVisual.com
Cover design by 1106 Design

DEDICATION

To my wife Mary,
and my children Liana, Tamaryn and Adam,
and my grandchildren Julian, Katrina and Madan,
who daily teach me about gratitude, love and joy.

ALSO BY WILLIAM R. YODER

The Possibility of an Ontology and Epistemology of Mysticism,
Ph.D. Dissertation, SUNY Buffalo, 1978.

Lighted Clearings for the Soul,
Alight Publications, New York, 2004.

Lighted Clearings of Possibility,
Alight Publications, New York, 2010.

Acknowledgements

I am very fortunate to have loving friends and family in my life who have, with humor and wisdom, encouraged and supported me on my journey. They continue to help me discover and become my deepest and best self.

In terms of the teachings and writings of others, this book is especially indebted to *A Course in Miracles* and to the work of Jerry and Esther Hicks and Abraham, Barry Neil Kaufman, Marianne Williamson and Gerald Jampolsky.

I am grateful to Jack Pendrak and Sallie Bakert for critiquing the early draft of this book. Their corrections and suggestions really helped me to clarify my vision.

I'd also like to thank the professionals who have been involved with this project. This includes Graham at Write To Your Market for the title and cover copy, and Michele and her whole team at 1106 Design for the beautiful cover graphics and elegant interior design. And a special thanks to Doran at 1106 Design for his editorial help, which combined a philosophical understanding of the material with a professional editor's publishing savvy.

Finally, I want to acknowledge my wife Mary. Her insightful and patient editing has (once again) been invaluable. Her comments and questions always challenge me to think harder, and bring a new level of clarity and depth to the finished work. And by her own example, she has taught me much about forgiveness, love and happiness.

TABLE OF CONTENTS

INTRODUCTION

Happiness is the promise and the goal of life. We are all looking for happiness. Happiness is much more than just a fleeting sense of feeling good. It includes feelings of fulfillment and deep satisfaction, the excitement of passionately pursuing and realizing your dreams, the deep peace of your innermost being, and the joy of unconditionally giving and receiving love. Happiness is more than just personal gratification and pleasure. We derive happiness from our kindness and compassion toward others, from service and generosity. And perhaps the deepest form of happiness comes from our spiritual journey, from our discovery of our loving connection with all of life. One's spiritual journey may or may not involve the teachings of an organized religion.

When we say that happiness is the promise and the goal of life, we have an ideal of perfect happiness, happiness that is consistent and lasting. But many of us experience only what we could call "imperfect" happiness—feelings of happiness that give way to unhappiness, moments of peace that give way to unpeace, experiences of well-being that give way to un-well-being. And thus every experience of happiness seems tentative and tenuous. There is a slight (or maybe even pronounced) undercurrent of fear and anxiety, because our good feelings and experiences may give way at any moment to unhappiness, loss, and suffering.

The Search

We are searching for some way to experience a deeper and more lasting kind of happiness. Happiness is, after all, the motivation and goal of everything we do. That is probably the reason you are reading this book now. A visit to your local bookstore or a quick search on the Internet will show you that happiness is one of the most popular topics today.

Some of the most publicized works today take a "just-think-positively-and-become-a-gazillionaire" approach. To those of us wanting more happiness and less fear and lack in our lives, these books seem to offer a quick and easy solution. Many people believe they are unhappy because they don't have enough of "the good stuff"—enough fame, power, or wealth to make their lives truly happy. These books promise us that if we merely follow a few simple techniques and do a few positive affirmations and visualizations, we will get or "manifest" everything we need to be happy.

I have several friends who are true believers in this approach. But from my perspective, it seems like their efforts to follow the formulas of their favorite books—such as reciting affirmations— are a little desperate. I say "desperate" because often there is an unpeaceful and grasping tone to their affirmations and other practices. It often sounds as if they think that they can't really be happy until they get the stuff they want, and they are a little bit afraid that the whole program might not work. And indeed, it doesn't always seem to work—at least for myself or the other people I have seen use it. Sometimes we get what we want, and sometimes we don't. Sometimes we get what we want, and then we lose it. Sometimes we get exactly what we don't want, what we were afraid might be coming to us. Maybe we were just not doing it quite right. Or maybe there is more to happiness than just repeating affirmations for the things you want. At any rate, I did not find that this method worked consistently for me.

The other problem with this approach is that deep down we all know that there is more to happiness than just getting stuff. It's not that the things of the world are somehow "bad," but simply that getting and having things is not enough for a truly happy, satisfying, fulfilling life. Having stuff is no guarantee of happiness. There are lots of rich and famous people who are unhappy, frightened, judgmental, unloving, unpeaceful, and insecure. Their unhappiness is not the fault of their riches or fame, since there are also rich and famous people who are genuinely happy. (Of course, we tend to tell ourselves that if *we* only had all that good stuff, then *we* would be quite happy. But I'm sure that the unhappy rich people told themselves that same thing while they were acquiring their wealth.)

There is also a whole class of books that make sweeping metaphysical claims about the "ultimate nature of reality" and the underlying "laws" governing the universe. I often find these books are very inspiring. But after my initial enthusiasm fades, I find myself asking, "How do I know that all of those claims are really true?" As a reflective and thoughtful person, I don't want to adopt a belief simply because it sounds noble and inspiring. I also need to understand the "why" behind the belief.

This book offers a unique approach to the topic of happiness. I say this not in criticism of the other books, since I myself have learned a great deal from them and I am grateful. But after years of study and searching, I wanted something more than I was able to find in the available writings and teachings on happiness.

That "Something More"

I wanted an approach that was thoughtful and intellectually sound, an approach that satisfied both my mind and my heart. I wanted more than mere claims about the nature of reality that I had to simply take on faith—I needed to understand the reason and rationale behind these claims. And I wanted more than a collection of practices and techniques—I needed to understand why I was following those practices and what they meant. But at the same time I wanted a down-to-earth approach that went beyond the merely theoretical, and actually worked for me in my own life. I wanted an approach that would move me closer to consistently experiencing happiness on a day-to-day basis; an approach that would allow me to shift from unpeace to peace, from unhappiness to happiness in any moment, regardless of circumstances, and an approach that would allow me to help others shift their own experience.

For me, the key issue is our core beliefs, and whether they are consistent with and supportive of perfect happiness. It is important to remember that we always have some core beliefs. Without them, we could not make sense of our lives at all, or purposely function in the world. So it's never a question of whether to have core beliefs. It's simply a matter of which core beliefs we choose—which core beliefs will best serve us and our world.

Many of the books available on happiness focus primarily on techniques such as positive affirmations and visualizations. They claim that if you do the right practices, in the right way, and do them often enough, it will eliminate the negativity in your life. The problem, however, is that if your underlying core beliefs necessarily give rise to unhappiness and other negative feelings, all of your visualizations and affirmations can't make a lasting change. This whole process of undermining our ability to be happy is subconscious, since none of us would deliberately choose unhappiness. Positive affirmations and visualizations can, of course, be a very valuable and powerful technique. But when our core beliefs are inconsistent with perfect happiness, then all of the positive affirmations and visualizations in the world can't give us what we truly want.

And even when these techniques succeed in "creating" or "manifesting" wealth and success in our lives, it will still not be enough if we have core beliefs that block our happiness—core beliefs that prevent us from recognizing and realizing the possibilities of love and joy and peace that life offers us. If we subconsciously maintain such core beliefs, then all the stuff in the world won't give us deep or lasting happiness. No matter how much we "succeed" and how much we acquire, our own minds will continue to sabotage themselves.

The Shift to One Power

Ultimately, most (or all) *unhappiness seems to be a reflection of a mind that is not at peace with itself, not secure in itself, not able to fully love itself or others.* That lack of peace is an *internal* condition of the mind, independent of external things and conditions. *To find deep and lasting happiness, we need to fundamentally change our awareness.* That means changing our core beliefs about ourselves and the world. And this is a deeper and more comprehensive process than simply repeating positive affirmations.

If our core beliefs are to provide a basis for harmony and peace of mind, they must be consistent within themselves. A set of conflicting and inconsistent core beliefs will give rise to an unpeaceful mind divided against itself. And an unpeaceful mind cannot be truly happy.

So what we need is a coherent and consistent *system* of beliefs. A consistent system of beliefs is one that is based on a single foundational principle. That one principle gives rise to all of the other beliefs in the system. Furthermore, that foundational belief must itself be undivided and consistent. If there is an inner conflict in the foundational principle, there will be conflict and inconsistency throughout all of the other beliefs. In other words, an inconsistent foundational principle cannot give rise to a consistent system of beliefs.

This book provides one possible system of beliefs, which I call seven principles for happiness. The foundational belief of this whole system is the principle of one power. As we go through what this principle means and all of its implications for our daily life, it may at times seem a little complex and abstract. But the principle of one power is very simple—in fact, it could be said that this principle is the very essence of simplicity. In the end, one power will turn out to be love itself—pure, unconditional, perfect love. And the ultimate value of the principle of one power is that it is deeply practical—it actually allows you to be happier moment by moment, to actually experience more peace, more joy, more love, more well-being in your life.

At times, this system of beliefs may seem challenging. That is because it seems to turn many of our everyday beliefs upside down. But we will discover that our usual way of thinking about ourselves and the world is actually quite inconsistent, and necessarily brings about feelings of unhappiness and fear. These everyday beliefs are so pervasive, however, that they are normally just taken for granted. We tend to think that it's "just the way it is," and we are unaware that there are any specific beliefs involved at all. Therefore, we tend to believe that unhappiness, fear, unpeace, loss, and suffering of every kind are simply a part of "how the world is." It is inevitable. You have to take the thorns with the roses. This is simply how things are.

A New Way of Thinking

These seven principles for happiness offer one possible alternative to our usual everyday beliefs. It is only when we consider an alternative system of beliefs that we can begin to see that our current beliefs are indeed just beliefs, just one possible interpretation of how things are. Then, for the first time, we arc in a position to deliberately choose our beliefs. Remember that you are not being asked to take any of these ideas on faith. They are simply possible belief choices that you can make if you want to. We will see how each of these beliefs can lead to a happier and more peaceful life. Just as importantly, we will see why choosing the opposite beliefs almost certainly leads to some degree of unhappiness and un-well-being.

Some may argue that the vision of human life I suggest in this book is too positive and is unrealistic. They would argue that the ideal of perfect happiness is impossible given all of the "imperfections" of human life on earth. They would argue that to pursue perfect happiness as a purpose or a goal would be self-deluding and dishonest at best, and selfish and morally irresponsible at worst. These and other similar objections sometimes masquerade as self-evident common sense truths. But once again they are actually based on core beliefs about the essence and nature of life—beliefs that are so pervasive and taken for granted that they no longer seem to be mere "beliefs" at all.

Remember throughout, however, that no matter how idealistic or lofty some of these ideas may sound, their real value to you is their down-to-earth practicality. They can actually allow you to experience a happier life on a day-to-day basis. They can actually allow you to forgive and love more fully. They can actually allow you to shift out of unhappiness into happiness in every moment, regardless of your circumstances. These ideas do work for me, and on a consistent basis. When I am living this system of beliefs, my life is happy and fulfilling, and it seems to have a beneficial effect on others. And whenever I am feeling some form of unpeace or unhappiness, I always find that I have slipped back into my previous beliefs, the everyday beliefs that I inherited from my culture, the beliefs that "everyone" seems to take for granted. As soon as I shift back into these seven principles for happiness—not just as a superficial repetition of a memorized formula, but truly shifting my mind—it always shifts my consciousness and my perception of myself and the world. This shift is always a shift of *healing,* and sometimes it seems miraculous. Fear gives way to love, unpeace gives way to peace, unhappiness gives way to happiness, conflict gives way to harmony, un-well-being gives way to well-being.

Will These Principles Work For *You?*

These are not the only possible principles for happiness, and it may not be necessary to consciously believe any or all of them in order to live a happy life. Perhaps being happy is as simple as just choosing to be happy. Maybe all you have to do is to follow your own inner guidance in order to be truly happy and to help others discover their own true happiness.

But when we have hidden our inner knowing under misleading beliefs, then we may need alternative ideas to help us undo those self-deceptive beliefs. The only time we really need any principles for happiness is when we are unhappy. These seven principles for happiness could be called seven principles of healing. They help us to undo those belief choices that make us unhappy, and to replace them with belief choices that allow our inner nature of happiness to shine forth. They help us to heal our experience of un-well-being and allow us to experience our underlying truth of perfect well-being.

The way of thinking presented in this book does not pretend to be an ultimate metaphysics, a supposedly accurate description of "how things really are." In fact, I don't believe that "how things really are" can be described by a conceptual theory at all. What ideas do is to create a kind of "lighted clearing" in our minds that allows us to experience certain possibilities and not others (for further discussion, see my book *Lighted Clearings for the Soul*). When our current ideas are limiting the possibilities we can experience, then we want to explore alternative ideas that can open our minds to deeper and richer possibilities.

Will these principles work for *you?* Will they allow *you* to experience a happier, more peaceful, and more loving life? Will they allow you to shift from unpeace to peace, from unhappiness to happiness in any moment, regardless of circumstances? For you to find out, you must actually *live* this system of beliefs. At the end of each chapter, there are three practical exercises. I encourage you to actually work through those exercises, in whatever form is best for you. These are practices that you will do more than once, that you incorporate into your day-to-day life and your relationships with others, on an on-going basis. It can be very helpful to keep a journal about what you discover about yourself and the world when you follow these practices.

There is nothing "wrong" with being unhappy or with experiencing un-well-being in our lives. I am not claiming that people "should" be happier and "should" experience more well-being in their lives. Nor am I suggesting in any way that we should blame ourselves or anyone else for whatever unhappiness or un-well-being we do experience. But I do believe that happiness is a more pleasant and healthier way to live our lives, a more effective way to realize our dreams. And our own happiness may be the greatest contribution we can make to the lives of others. I hope and trust that this book will help you to discover and maintain a deeper and more consistent level of happiness in your life, for your sake and for the sake of all those whose life and happiness is tied to your own.

PRINCIPLE ONE
ONE POWER

*There is only one power. That power is
the infinite eternal creative potential
for ever-expanding well-being.*

As I said in the Introduction (which you should read before starting this chapter), the principle of one power is basically very simple. Ultimately it is this very simplicity that holds this system of thought together as a whole and provides a touchstone for all of our other belief choices. It is this principle that will be the very foundation of experiencing happiness and healing and well-being in every area of your life.

The first principle is that there is *only one power*, one source of all that is. The key here is to understand the simplicity of this principle. There is only *one* power—not two powers, not three powers, not several powers, only one power.

This power is not neutral, like a battery. The one power of this first principle is love itself—pure, unconditional, perfect love.

So that's the first principle, the foundational principle which holds together this entire system of thought that can radically transform our lives: there is only one power, and that power is love.

At first glance, however, the principle of one power seems inconsistent with our experience. We actually experience contrast and difference all the time. This difference often is experienced as a conflict between two powers: a power for good and a power for bad, a power for our benefit and a power for our harm. Moreover, to say that love is the source of all things seems overly idealistic and unrealistic. What about all of the suffering we experience—the lack, the conflict, the fear, the sickness and deterioration, the wars and economic recessions? All of these things certainly don't seem to be expressions of perfect love. Obviously our new belief system can't simply ignore our actual experience.

But as we explore these ideas more deeply, we will discover that our underlying beliefs may be the real cause of our experience of suffering, rather than some external reality made up of forces and powers that are threatening our well-being. In particular, the primary cause of our experience of suffering is the underlying belief that I call the belief in two powers (i.e., the belief that there is more than one power). I say "underlying," since for the most part we are not aware that we hold that belief at all. The belief in two powers is perhaps the most pervasive belief in human thought, and it seems to sneak in everywhere. It is so pervasive that it is not often even recognized as a belief at all. It is merely presumed that the existence of two powers is simply the way things are. The *belief* in two powers is the *belief* that there is more than creative love at play in our lives. It is the *belief* that there are other powers and forces that threaten our happiness and well-being, whether intentionally (such as other people trying to harm us) or unintentionally (such as germs and viruses making us sick). It is the *belief* that these other powers and forces can cause us harm and loss and suffering, and we are, at least to some extent, at their mercy.

Yes, we do experience conflict and fear and suffering. But our question here is whether the experience of suffering is inevitable—whether the *experience* of suffering is an intrinsic part of the very fabric of reality, or is simply a reflection of our beliefs. Virtually all mystical spiritual traditions claim that suffering is *not* inevitable. They claim that it is possible to shift our level of consciousness and eliminate suffering from our experience. This first principle of one power can be a valuable tool in making that shift—a valuable tool in undoing or eliminating the experience of conflict and fear caused by our belief in two powers.

Source is Love

The principle of one power is that there is only one power, and that power is love. To say that this one power is love means that it is *the infinite eternal creative potential for ever-expanding well-being.*

To say that source is love means that source is pure positive energy, which eternally expresses itself as ever-expanding well-being. Well-being includes well-being in every area of life experience: peace, joy, abundance, harmony, fullness, and wholeness. To say that this source is the only power means that the eternal creative flow toward ever-expanding goodness is the essence and truth of all reality, and the essence and truth of every now.

To call this one power *creative* means that source, in its own nature, is eternally creating, eternally expanding itself. Source includes its creative expressions as part of its being. Source, in its own nature, *is* the creative potential, the creating, and the creative expressions. And beyond source there is nothing.

This doesn't mean that there is some limit to source, and that just beyond that limit we would find some vast empty space. It means that beyond source there is nothing, nothing at all. There *is* only source. Source is the very foundation, essence and truth of is-ness itself.

Source "creates" by extending or sharing itself. That means that everything-that-is is an extension of this source—to *be* means to be an expression of source. Since source is love, everything-that-is is an expression of love. Everything and everyone shares the same truth, the same essence, the same content: love.

Some people prefer to call this one power, this one source, by the name of "God." For myself personally, I am very comfortable with the word "God." But I am choosing here to use the more neutral term "source," because "God" is often understood to mean a transcendent being that is separate from the world and from ourselves.

The "one power" or "one source," however, is not a "being" at all. Rather it is more like the very Being-ness of all beings, the very is-ness of all that is. Source is not separate from beings. Source creatively expresses itself *as* beings, and beings *are* the extensions of source.

This idea of source might correspond to a more mystical or non-dualistic conception of God. But it would not be synonymous with the "God" of any dualistic thought system of "God plus something else" (for instance, God and the world, or God and you). Source, as we are using the term, means that beyond which there is nothing. And so there is no "something else" it could possibly be separate from.

The creative process of extension that gives rise to everything-that-is is *eternal*. In this context, "eternal" does not mean lasting a long long time into some distant forever. Here, "eternal" means *always already now*. Creation is not some event in the distant past, nor is your own creation an event that happened twenty or thirty or sixty years ago. The first principle implies that you are being "created" or "sourced" *now*, moment by moment. Your very being *is* an extending-forth of the one source now.

This means that you, in your very truth, are a be-ing of the infinite potential for well-being, a be-ing of pure positive energy, a be-ing of the creative expansion of Love. I am using the hyphenated spelling of "be-ing" to emphasize that you are a creative *process* rather than a mere thing. Your very be-ing is an individualized expression of the eternal creative process of the very lov-ing of Love Itself—the on-going extending-forth of peace, joy, and well-being. This is your eternal truth and essence, even when your thoughts and beliefs hide it from your own awareness.

The Experience of Contrast and Difference

As we noted, the principle of one power seems to fly in the face of our everyday experience. We experience a world of contrasts and differences. In fact, our bodily senses perceive only by contrast—for instance, you can see the bright star only against the black sky. Our conceptual thinking is based on difference. To "de-fine" something means to draw a boundary between what it is and what it is not.

We tend to experience all of this contrast and difference not merely as a rich diversity, but in terms of better and worse. And so we experience a world of abundance and lack, of health and sickness, of peace and conflict, of happiness and unhappiness. In short, we experience a world that seems to be driven by two powers: a power for good and a power for bad, a power for well-being and a power for un-well-being. Furthermore, we also experience a world that seems to be made up of two different kinds of reality: for instance, mind and body, the inner world and the outer world, spirit and matter. And each reality seems to have its own independent power.

This interpretation of difference in terms of opposing powers is reflected as a pervasive sense of conflict and struggle in our lives. Since we experience ourselves as separate and different from everything else, we tend to experience our lives as an on-going battle between ourselves and others—a battle of trying to get what we want from others, and trying to defend ourselves when others try to take from us. We may experience an on-going struggle with the world—for instance, a struggle against adverse political and economic forces, or a struggle against bacteria and viruses and other forces of disease. We may even experience a struggle with our own bodies, when a sick or failing body seems to keep us from enjoying our lives and doing what we want.

We may experience this difference and contrast in our lives as a conflict between the forces of good and evil. Sometimes this may take the form of battling the forces of evil in the world. Other times, it may take the form of an inner battle between a "good self" and a "bad self"—between our desire to be forgiving and loving, and the temptation to do or say something unkind when outer forces seem to push us to our limits.

Our sense of conflict can give rise to a feeling of guilt or shame. When we see the world in terms of conflict and competition between ourselves and others, it seems necessary to sometimes attack others, either to defend ourselves or to get what we need. When we give in to the temptation to lash out and be hurtful, or to the temptation to get something for ourselves at the expense of another, we feel uneasy. We may feel a sense of guilt or shame for simply entertaining selfish or greedy or unkind thoughts, even if we don't act them out. Some religions actually promote a sense of guilt, claiming that you are indeed "sinful" and separate from God and thus you "should" feel guilty. For those religions, acknowledging and owning your own "truth of guilt" is the necessary first step in your religious journey of "salvation."

The pervasive sense of conflict also gives rise to an on-going undercurrent of fear. There is the fear that another might triumph over you; the fear that you might triumph over another (and thus be guilty); the fear that you might not get what you need; the fear that you might get what you don't want; the fear that you might lose what you have; the fear of some kind of punishment or karmic repayment for your mistakes and failings; the fear of loss and lack, sickness and injury; and ultimately, the fear of death (and perhaps even the fear of some form of punishment or damnation after death).

Of course, most of us do not feel embattled all of the time. We don't feel a continuous sense of guilt and fear. We do have our happy moments, our times of loving, and our experiences of beauty. But these experiences occur within the context of their opposites. Within a world of two powers, each moment of peace is only a temporary and tenuous intermission in the overall battle of life.

We tend to resign ourselves to this sense of conflict and guilt and fear. We tell ourselves, "You have to take the bad with the good." We even rationalize this kind of experience and argue that it has positive value. We say, "You couldn't really appreciate a sunny day unless you had rainy ones."

The Question of the "Reality of Evil"

We do in fact find ourselves in the midst of a life experience defined by contrast and difference, a life experience of a mixture of good and bad, of well-being and un-well-being. In theological terms, you could say that we find ourselves in the midst of experiencing a mixture of both the Godly and the ungodly in our lives. Within this context of experience, a (or perhaps the) crucial question to ask ourselves is how will we *choose to* interpret our perceptions of badness—our perceptions of evil, of guilt, of being unfairly treated, of victimhood, of loss and lack, of sickness and pain, of death.

Basically, we have two alternatives. We could choose to interpret our perceptions of the bad that we experience in our lives as true perceptions of a real power for badness. In other words, we would think that conflict and fear and suffering were an intrinsic part of reality itself. This would be an expression of what we called the belief in two powers.

Or, we could choose to remain steadfast in our belief in one power. We could choose to understand every perception of badness as merely the temporary hiddenness of the underlying truth of goodness. We could choose to understand every perception of badness as merely a temporary distortion of our experience caused by our own limited and limiting ideas of goodness—ultimately, a distortion caused by our choice to believe in two powers.

But wouldn't it be foolishly one-sided to believe in only one power? If you chose to believe only in the reality of good, and to not believe in the reality of bad, wouldn't you merely be hiding half of the truth from yourself? Wouldn't you be simplistic and naïve, ignoring the harsh realities of life and seeing everything through rose-colored glasses?

There is no simple answer to this objection. If there really were two powers, then to merely ignore one of them would indeed be one-sided, and would hide half of the truth from yourself.

But if there really were only one power, then to believe in two powers would be to hide the *whole* truth from yourself.

Within a two-power or dualistic thought system, "good" means a conditional and limited good—a good that is co-defined with bad. "Good" *means* "not bad." That is *not* the same good as the unconditional and non-relative good inherent in the principle of one power, a good beyond which there is nothing. If there really is only one power, then your belief in the reality of a limited relative "good" would effectively block you from experiencing the unconditional and non-relative good, would effectively block your awareness of the presence of perfect love.

Ultimately, whether or not there is some "what really is" apart from your beliefs and experiences—and that may be an unanswerable question—your beliefs do limit and define your experience. The "cost" of the belief in one power would be relinquishing your feelings of fear and guilt. The "cost" of your belief in two-powers would be giving up the very possibility of experiencing perfect happiness. The question for you here is how do *your* beliefs limit and define *your* experience?

An Either-Or Choice

You have to choose to believe either in one power, OR in more than one power. These two choices are mutually exclusive. Moreover, you will always be making one of these choices, and your choice will be expressed in how you think about your current situation, how you experience it, and how you respond to it.

It may seem that it is always better to choose a both-and alternative over an either-or one. We strive to be inclusive rather than exclusive.

But you cannot believe in *only one* power and at the same time in more than one power. When you perceive anything that is seemingly bad, you have to choose whether to believe that it is really bad (i.e., an expression of some real power for badness), OR to believe that it is merely your temporary inability to see the truth of its underlying goodness. You have to choose whether to think that the belief in only one power is merely naive, OR is the most truthful and revealing belief choice possible. You cannot choose both.

This is not a belief choice that you make one time, once and for all. You are implicitly making it in every moment of your life. You may choose to believe in one power in one moment or one situation or one relationship, and then choose to believe in two powers in the next. You will know which choice you are making by how you feel.

It may seem difficult to seriously consider the principle of one power, when it seems that all of your current experience so clearly demonstrates that there is more than one power. As we said, we do in fact experience conflict and suffering; we do in fact experience our lives as an expression of two opposing powers. We experience our lives as a kind of battle between the forces for our well-being and the forces that would threaten or harm our well-being. From that perspective, the idea that there is only the power of love—a creative power for the well-being of all—seems to be just plain foolish.

Our beliefs define and determine both what we can experience and how we can experience it. So the real question is not so much, "what is my current experience, and what beliefs should I adopt based on that experience?" It is rather, "what beliefs are being reflected in and as my current experience?" And even more importantly, "what kinds of beliefs would be reflected as the kinds of experience that I truly desire?"

Any time we are trying to fundamentally change our experience, we will need to begin to believe and practice new principles that seem inconsistent with our current experience. And this is done in the faith that once we are actually living our new beliefs, they will begin to influence and change our experience. So the question here is: Are you perfectly happy with your current experience? If you are not, then you may find it necessary to consider new beliefs that are inconsistent with your current experience. Now, what may seem somewhat paradoxical is that it is only by actually living the new beliefs that you gain the experiences that validate and justify those beliefs. But, fortunately, you don't have to wait too long. If you really keep your eyes open, each little step you take will be reflected in new experiences—seemingly serendipitous events that confirm your new choices and suggest the next step.

Any feeling of unpeace—including anger, sadness, fear, guilt, hatred, or unhappiness—is always a reflection of an underlying belief in two powers. This belief in two powers may be expressed in many different ways: you versus another, you versus a body which you experience as sick or injured, you versus germs or viruses or pollution, you versus economic or political forces that seem to threaten you, you versus the world, or even you versus God. Or you may think of this conflict as some cosmic battle of good and evil, or of God and Satan.

When you choose to believe in two powers, you will imagine that you feel unpeace *because* of some real battle, whether you think of it as a battle between you and something else, or as a battle between some larger power for good and some larger power for bad. But the real cause of your experience of unpeace in any situation is ultimately your own belief in two powers.

What you feel is always a reflection of what thoughts you are thinking—what thoughts you are **choosing** *to think.*

If you are committed to believe that there is only one power, and that power is the infinite eternal creative potential for goodness and love, then you know there can never be any real reason to feel upset in any way. Even when you seem to experience evil or lack or suffering in yourself or others, you will choose to interpret it as only a temporary distortion of your perception. You will choose to respond with compassion and love, without fear or anger or hatred or despair. *Peace is the reflection of the belief in one power.*

Beyond Technique

Many of the books and teachings available on happiness provide you with various techniques and affirmation formulas. These are designed to help you navigate your way through the perilous journey called human life. They are tools you can use to manipulate the world and others, to get (or perhaps "manifest") the things that you want, to ward off danger, to make yourself feel happy whenever you are depressed or afraid, to make you feel safe whenever you are insecure. These tools and techniques provide a temporary haven from the stress of life. The implicit assumption is that the journey really is perilous, that life really is stressful. The implicit assumption is that what we perceive as bad in the world really is bad—that there is some real force or power in play that will thwart your well-being and your happiness if you are not careful. And for that reason, we need various tools and techniques to keep ourselves safe, and to somehow create those things and conditions that make our lives better and enable us to live "the good life."

There is always a level of fear involved in such a process. We have to keep following those techniques, keep repeating those affirmations. If we don't do enough, then the dangers of life will overcome us and we will suffer lack and loneliness and poor health and every other form of un-well-being. We have to keep following the correct techniques (and there is some disagreement about which ones those are), and we have to do them exactly right. The stress and the perils of life never rest. I have one good friend who reads virtually all of the popular self-help books, always looking for a new technique, a new affirmation. He is always sharing some new phrase or formula from the latest book, and telling me that this one really works. Even when I discussed the principle of one power with him, he simply took that as one more technique. Whenever he felt stressed or afraid, he would repeat the mantra, "There is only one power and that power is love." Basically he was using the first principle as a kind of magical amulet to ward off threat and danger. But all of this came from the conviction that the dangers and the threats he was warding off were real. The principle of one power was reduced to an affirmation formula that he used within his core belief system of two powers.

This is an example of what I would call a "technique approach" to life and happiness. I think that this is very prevalent in our culture, and is what creates the demand for so many technique-based self-help books. I am not criticizing the use of techniques. In fact, I believe that any theoretical approach must be complemented by some kind of practical exercises if it is to have a real effect on your life experience. But I don't think that techniques by themselves are enough to change your life from fear to love, especially if they are practiced from within a belief system of two powers. Even the mere technique of repeating the phrase "there is only one power" is not enough. We have heard people (perhaps even ourselves) claim in one breath that "all is love," and complain about struggle and lack and suffering in the next.

What I call "the belief in the reality of evil" is pervasive and insidious, not just in our culture but in virtually every culture. In Genesis, we are told that we were expelled from the Garden of Eden because we ate the fruit of the tree of the knowledge of good and evil. Many people take this at face value, believing that once we disobeyed God by learning about real evil, we were condemned to a life of real suffering.

But from the perspective of a belief in one power, there could be another way to understand that story. It could be interpreted as an explanation of where our *experience* of suffering really came from. If God is the only source and power, and God is all-good, then there can be no evil. That would mean that the phrase "the knowledge of good and evil" really referred to an illusory belief in two powers, the illusory belief in both good and evil, the illusory belief that evil was real. So humans, by adopting the (mistaken) belief in two powers, moved themselves out of that place in their minds of perfect love and peace and happiness, and became locked into an (ultimately illusory) experience of suffering and fear. From that perspective, the whole idea of a vengeful God expelling us from perfect happiness is simply a projection, blaming God for what we did to ourselves. Making God "vengeful" was projecting a kind of dualism onto God. God's love was no longer unconditional. It had now become merely conditional—we would be loved as long as we followed the rules (were good), but would be punished if we strayed (were bad).

We see some version of this story in most of the world's religions. The idea of the reality of evil and the inevitability of suffering seems to be a belief in most or all of human culture. But all of the mystics from virtually every spiritual tradition claim that evil is not truly real, and suffering is not inevitable. What needs to change is not the world, but our own minds.

The technique approach to life tends to be based on the belief that we must somehow manipulate life in order to be happy and safe. But perhaps life doesn't need to be manipulated for us to be happy. Perhaps the belief that it needs to be manipulated is itself the problem. Perhaps our desperate attempt to manipulate life is exactly what blinds us to knowing a deeper truth of love. The alternative is not mere passivity but rather insightful action based on inner knowing. Perhaps what we really need to do is to reconnect with our own inner truth of joy.

I believe that the real importance of understanding and practicing these seven principles for happiness is to eventually lead you to a place where you *know*—not just think, but know—that there is only one power and that power is love. "Know" in this context means more than just intellectual and conceptual knowledge. This knowing is a direct experience, rather than a thought. It is an inner certainty deep within your being. The real purpose of these seven principles is to lead you to that place of knowing within your own inner being. If you truly know that there is only one power and that power is love, that inner knowing will dissipate your fears—your fear of loss, of suffering, of being threatened, of being unfairly treated. Because if you *know* that there is only love, then there is nothing to fear. You realize that your fears are simply a temporary forgetfulness of the truth of perfect love. You realize that your perception of the peril and threats and dangers of human life is merely a temporary distortion based on falling back into a mistaken belief in two powers. And you know that such a belief is mistaken, because from that place of inner vision you know with certainty that there is only one power and that power is love.

So the ultimate goal of this book is more than simply to provide you with new techniques and affirmations to help you "cope with" life. The goal is to provide the ideas and practical tools which, when combined with your own innate understanding, can serve as a road map into a deeper level of your own truth. This goal may seem presumptuous and idealistic to some readers. But I think that nothing less will lead to a deep and lasting happiness that is not at the mercy of circumstances. And nothing less would be worthy of who you are. But remember that it is not enough to merely understand the road map—to really get anywhere, you must actually take that inner journey yourself.

Practicing the Principle of One Power

When you experience something in your life that seems un-source-like—for instance, wrong, bad, tragic, unfair, threatening, fearful, or painful—choose to look at it as the temporary hiddenness of source in your awareness. Ask a deeper part of your mind to allow you to see it with the eyes of love. How does this transform your perception? How does your transformed perception affect how you feel?

In every moment, try to focus your attention on the underlying truth of every event and every being you experience. Try to see each one as an expression of the infinite eternal creative potential for well-being. Look for the underlying impulse toward ever-expanding goodness. Try to look beneath your own judgments and fears, and see each being as an expression of the truth of love itself. When you look with different eyes and a different mind, does it change what you are able to see?

The first part of this practice is a meditative exercise. Set aside a quiet time without distractions. Affirm for yourself, "I am now a be-ing of the one infinite, eternal, creative power of love. My being is the very lov-ing of love itself, the on-going creative extending-forth of peace and joy and well-being." (If these particular words don't feel exactly right to you, make whatever changes are appropriate as long as you keep the basic meaning.) Don't just say the words, but try to actually *experience* the idea, to actually experience *being* the very lov-ing of love itself, *being* the extending-forth of peace and joy and well-being.

In the second part of the exercise, take some time to consider the situations or circumstances in your life which you believe to be the source of any feelings of unhappiness or fear you may be experiencing. Make a list of those situations. Address them one at a time. As you think through each one, sink into the experience of yourself as a be-ing of the infinite creative power of love. Does this change how you think, and more importantly, how you feel about yourself in this situation?

Finally, you can use this affirmation as a helpful reminder of who you are when you find yourself experiencing a stressful situation.

REMINDER: It can be very helpful to keep a journal about your experiences when you do these practices. In the very act of figuring out how to express and communicate your experiences (in prose or poetry or some other creative form), you will deepen your understanding of your own unique journey and truth.

PRINCIPLE TWO
CREATIVE MIND

*Your mind is an individualized
expression of creative source.
Creative mind creates by creating
ideas, and then translating those ideas
into concrete experience. Your life
experience is the reflection of those
ideas that you have created and
have chosen to believe.*

Our minds play a *creative* role in our experience of the world, influencing what we experience, how we experience it, and how we feel about it. Our experience and our feelings aren't merely "given," or determined by some external reality. In fact, we have a great deal more creative input in the process than most people imagine. This is actually very good news, because it means that we can determine, to a large extent, our own happiness. By deliberately choosing our beliefs and thoughts, we can create or co-create the kinds of feelings and experiences we want. In this chapter, we will explore the creative power of our minds, and will look at which kinds of thoughts and beliefs give rise to happy feelings and experiences. We will discover that many of our everyday beliefs that we take for granted actually make us unhappy. Understanding this will allow us to choose new beliefs and become *conscious co-creators* of our experience.

The second principle is the principle of creative mind. The principle of creative mind is ultimately based on our first principle of one power. These two principles together are the theoretical foundation of our thought system. The rest of the principles are down-to-earth and lead to the very practical goal of a happier life. But for those practical principles to really make sense for you, you have to understand the first two principles they are based on. And as I said in the previous chapter, this means much more than a merely intellectual understanding. You want to actually *experience* yourself and the world through the perspective offered by these first two principles.

The principle of one power is simply that there is only one power or source, and that power is love. Love is the infinite eternal creative potential for ever-expanding well-being. Source creates by extending itself.

The second principle specifies what source creates, what source extends itself as. Source creates or extends itself as creative mind. To understand the idea of "creative mind," we have to explain both what "mind" means and how mind "creates."

To know what creative mind is, you have only to look at your own mind. Creative mind exists in the form of individualized expressions of mind. The individualized expressions of mind—for instance, my mind or your mind—are not separate pieces or fragments of creative mind. Each individualized mind is an expression of the whole of creative mind.

For this thought system, "your mind" means your *whole sphere of awareness.* Your mind is not an object of awareness, but is rather the *creative self-aware openness* within which *all* of the objects of your awareness come and go. The objects of your awareness include the so-called mental or inner objects of awareness such as thoughts and feelings, as well as the sensations, such as colors and shapes and sounds, that you usually associate with bodies and the outer world. In this sense, "mind" is not the opposite of "body," but is rather the self-aware openness within which all of your mental and physical experiences exist. Experientially understanding the distinction between awareness and the objects of awareness is crucial here.

Therefore, "your mind" does not refer to that little fragment of consciousness that is somehow encased in your head, and is somehow conditioned and defined by your body. It is the whole sphere of awareness, within which you experience the whole drama of "a separate consciousness riding around in a body."

Likewise, your mind or awareness is different from the "you" that is defined by a certain personality and personal history, certain traits, tendencies, patterns and habits of thinking and responding. That "you" is just one of the objects of your awareness, one of the ideas and experiences that exists within the openness of your awareness.

According to the principle of one power, everything-that-is is an extension of source, and thus shares its qualities and characteristics. Source eternally extends itself as creative mind, which exists as individualized mind. You, as an individualization of mind, *are* an extension of the one source. Your mind *is* an individualized be-ing of source.

Source is love, the infinite eternal creative potential for well-being. Mind, as an extension of source, is an expression of this infinite eternal creative potential for well-being. The way that creative mind "creates" is by creating thoughts and creatively translating them into experience. Your mind is an individualized expression of creative mind. You, in your truth, *are* one be-ing, one expression, of the eternal creative expansion of source, which exists as the eternal creating of thoughts and experiences.

Your Experience Reflects Your Thoughts

Your mind is a self-aware process of creating thoughts, which take concrete form as your experiences. Your beliefs determine where you focus your attention. They determine how you interpret what you experience, its meaning and significance for you. They determine how you feel about what you experience and how you respond to it. Your experience of the world is a reflection or re-presentation of your thoughts and ideas.

That means that your experience of the world is never just a picture of some reality "out there" that your body's senses have simply delivered to your mind. Your body's senses do not sense meaning or value. The contribution of your body's senses includes your experiences of colors and shapes and sounds and textures. Then your mind *makes* sense of all of these sensations, interpreting them *as* sensations of a *meaningful* world. You experience your life in terms of beings related to one another in meaningful situations—even if occasionally the only meaning that you perceive is "meaninglessness" or "randomness." At every step of the way, your mind *brings* to your experience *all* of the meaning that your experience has for you. Your world—the world *you experience*—*is* a reflection of your thoughts.

I am emphasizing the world "you experience" to make it clear that we are not talking about the world "in itself." What the world is in itself, or whether there is any particular world in itself apart from all awareness, may well be unanswerable questions. Here we are talking about the world as it exists in your experience. And your experience of the world is always *interpreted* experience.

All of the meaning that you "find" in your experience is meaning that your mind has brought to that experience. The thoughts that you send forth are received back by you in the form of the reflected experiences. In the sphere of your own awareness, you receive exactly what you give; you reap exactly what you sow.

This is not to say that you are rewarded for "good" thoughts and punished for "bad" ones. The world you experience *is* the reflection of your thoughts. Your thoughts and their reflections exist simultaneously in your awareness, just as you and your image in the mirror exist simultaneously. In creative mind, a thought, precisely in being a thought, is being creatively translated into an experiential reflection. That is how a thought exists.

Source-like and Un-source-like Thoughts

Your mind creatively translates your thoughts into experiences. We can distinguish between two kinds of thoughts: source-like thoughts and un-source-like thoughts. Source-like thoughts are thoughts of one power, of well-being, of love and happiness and abundance in every area of life. Un-source-like thoughts include thoughts of two powers, thoughts of the restriction or limitation of well-being, thoughts of un-well-being, thoughts of conflict and threat.

Source-like thoughts will be reflected as experiences of well-being and feelings of happiness. Un-source-like thoughts will be reflected as experiences of un-well-being and lack, and feelings of unhappiness.

When your mind self-awarely extends forth only thoughts of unconditional love and well-being, it perceives only the reflection of love and well-being. But when you are unaware of your truth and believe that you are separate, limited and vulnerable, you will extend forth only limited and conditional love. Then you will perceive reflections of limited love and limited well-being. This means that you will experience a world with seemingly real forces of un-love and un-well-being, seemingly real forces of evil and suffering, sickness and lack.

In the most general terms, every un-source-like idea is based on the belief that there is something that is separate from source.

That would mean that source itself is somehow limited. When your mind believes that there is some limitation to the creative potential for pure well-being, that idea will be reflected as your experience of limited well-being.

The limitation of well-being is never experienced as a mere absence of well-being in your experience, as if there is simply a hole or a gap where some well-being should be. The belief in the limitation of well-being is always reflected as your experience of some seemingly real un-well-being—some seemingly real evil, guilt, suffering, lack or sickness. The belief in the limitation of goodness will be experienced as the apparently real presence of badness, the so-called "reality of evil."

In short, any belief in the limitation of source will be reflected as the experience of a world that is a *mixture* of source and not-source, of well-being and un-well-being, of good and bad. The experience of a world of two powers is a reflection of your belief in two powers.

Ultimately, the creative power in any experience is source itself, since source is the only power. *All* your experience is the result of a *co-creative* process of source's creative power expressing itself through your thoughts. Your source-like thoughts allow the manifestation of source-like experiences of abundance and love and joy. In a sense, you share the credit for your source-like experiences, since you chose the allowing thoughts that made those experiences possible for you. Your un-source-like thoughts, however, restrict and distort the manifestation of source, giving rise to the illusion of un-source-like things and forces. The negative aspects of your experience—the illusions of lack and darkness and un-well-being—are *entirely of your own making*, since source itself is contributing only love. Experiences of fear and guilt and suffering are only a reflection of the awareness which is doing the experiencing—its openness or closed-off-ness to love—and not a reflection of the possibilities being offered by source.

It is important to realize you are not "allowing" or "restricting" source itself. That would imply that you were a second power that could somehow act in opposition to source-power. What you are actually allowing or restricting is *your own awareness of source*—the extent to which your own awareness is allowed to manifest source-power in the form of experiences of well-being. Allowing or restricting the manifestation of source means allowing or restricting the mind that is doing the manifesting, and never the source that is being manifested.

Metaphorically speaking, any darkness that you perceive in your world is only a reflection of the limitation of light that you are extending. It is only a reflection of the dark and unloving thoughts that you are thinking, thoughts of limitation and neediness and vulnerability. Your thoughts of separation are reflected as experiences of conflict and threat, and feelings of anger and fear.

Likewise, any light you perceive in your world is a reflection of the light and loving thoughts you are extending, thoughts of wholeness and well-being. The light you perceive is a reflection of the light you are *allowing* to shine through you—that is to say, the light you are allowing your own mind to be aware of. But the light of source continues to shine, regardless of whether you are choosing to open your eyes or to close them.

In terms of happiness, this means that you can never credit your own happiness, or blame your own unhappiness, on something outside your awareness. What each thing or situation means to you is the meaning that you yourself have given to it.

If you experience something in the world that seems to "make" you happy, it is because *you* have given it a happy or lovable meaning—you have chosen thoughts and beliefs that allow your mind to be aware of the source-truth of that experience. A happy experience of the world *is* a reflection of seeing the world from a happy state of mind. Conversely, if you are upset about something in the world, what you are really upset about is *your own* interpretation of it. Whatever relative goodness or badness you "find" in your experience is a reflection of the meaning that your own mind has contributed.

According to the principles of one power and creative mind, there is no real power of darkness. The notion that there really is something external to mind that could be light or dark "in itself"—even this is just a thought. In your actual experience, there are only the reflections of the thoughts and meanings you are extending.

That means that the only true healing response to any perceived darkness—to any experience of guilt, sickness, suffering, loss or lack—is to extend more love and light. Extending more love and light means being willing to allow more love and light to extend through you. You do this by being willing to let go of your limiting beliefs and fears and judgments that are restricting your ability to co-creatively manifest source's infinite potential for perfect well-being. The effect of extending more light is that your own mind becomes aware of more light in its own experiences.

If, however, I try to solve a "problem" situation by somehow attacking and fighting against the darkness, I will just further limit my own experience of well-being. The fear or anger or hatred involved in any attack is a limitation of the love I am extending. Any time I regard the darkness as real, I will remain in a state of mind of fear or anger or hatred, which will be creatively translated as the experience of a world of cruelty and injustice, a world of scarcity and suffering. In my own withholding of love, I will be making for myself a dream-world of darkness.

At the same time my mind is generating its own interpreted experience—either co-creating experiences of well-being, or making experiences of un-well-being—it is also influencing other minds. When others see me battling against the darkness, it will tend to reinforce their own beliefs in the reality of darkness. When others see me extending unconditional love, it will reinforce awareness of their own capacity to do so. What I choose will not "cause" others to have specific beliefs or experiences. But it can influence them to look for and experience either more light or more darkness in their own lives.

Ultimately what you offer to another in any interaction is your own state of mind. Even in an interaction when you offer something concrete to another person, such as material assistance or words of kindness, what you are really giving to the other is the state of mind of your offering.

For instance, when you give money to another person, you can do it either out of a state of mind of fear and lack, or out of a state of mind of abundance. A state of mind of fear and lack might include "giving to get"—thinking you will get some kind of return for your "generosity." Or you might believe that you have a moral obligation to share your wealth with those who seem needy and deprived. Or perhaps you think that your giving can somehow atone for your past "sins" and "bad karma," and help you escape future punishment. You may even be giving out of a genuine desire to be helpful but believe that you have to have less so that others can have more.

In these examples, you are thinking of your giving as a form of self-sacrifice. You are also thinking of the other person as limited and needy and vulnerable. In doing so, you are implicitly affirming the reality of fear and scarcity in your own mind. And what you are truly giving to the other is the reinforcement of his own beliefs in fear and scarcity and lack.

The alternative is to be kind or generous out of abundance, out of the consciousness that you are an expression of infinite creative source. You know that you cannot suffer any loss or lack as a result of your generosity. You know that all of the abundance in your own experience is a reflection of source's infinite potential for well-being, which you are co-creatively allowing to manifest in your life. And what you are truly giving or sharing with the other is the state of mind of abundance, love and peace. By not reinforcing her ideas of limitation and lack, you are helping her to more fully allow the truth of well-being to dawn in her own awareness.

Every experience of unhappiness is ultimately a reflection of some limitation of your own extension of love and happiness. This limitation appears as the seemingly real presence of unloving and unhappy events and circumstances in your experience of the world. The only way to receive love and happiness from the world is to extend loving and happy thoughts to the world. *Your happy experiences do not cause you to be happy. Your happy experiences are the creative manifestation of your happy thoughts.*

The Thought of an External World

According to the first principle of one power, everything-that-is is an extension of source. That means that you are, in your truth, an extension of source itself. You are not separate or different from source. You *are* an individualized be-ing of source.

But you can choose to *believe* that you are somehow separate and apart from source. The idea of separateness is the idea of externality—if you are separate from source, source is somehow external to you. Believing in the idea of your own separateness will be creatively translated as the experience of a seemingly external world. This is a world that is beyond your control, a world that simply happens "to" you. It is a world that determines what you experience and how you feel, a world that victimizes you. Your thought of separation (ultimately, your separation from source or love) has been creatively translated into the experience of "living in an external world that seems to cause your experiences."

In effect, creative mind has created the illusion for itself that it is not creative but merely reactive—the illusion that it is passive and vulnerable, at least to some degree, to external forces and laws over which it has no control. This is fundamentally an experience of "you versus everything else"—an experience of resistance and struggle, an experience of threat and fear.

From the one-power perspective, the very idea of "separation" is meaningless. There is nothing beyond source that source could be separate from. Even the creative expressions of source are ultimately only extensions of source. They are not separate or different from source, nor are they essentially different from one another. And since there is no fragmentation within source, no gaps or holes, there is no separation possible within source either.

But even though the idea of separation is meaningless, a free creative mind can choose to take it seriously. Your mind can pretend that the definition of separation makes sense. Indeed, this may even have a certain attraction for you, because you may like the idea that you are separate and different from everything else—you may like the idea that you are somehow "special."

When you take the idea of separateness seriously, your creative mind creatively translates it into an *experience* of separateness. That's what creative mind does—it creatively thinks thoughts, and creatively translates those thoughts into experience. Even if an idea is essentially meaningless, creative mind will find a way to translate it into experience. You will believe and experience yourself to be separate from the source of all life. You will perceive yourself as separate from an external world of physical bodies. Bodies (including your own body) are, by definition, separate from one another and are external to mind. These bodies exist in space and time, which are experiential dimensions of externality—dimensions that allow one thing or event to be experienced as external to another. Space separates here from there; time separates now from then, the present from the past and the future.

Once you believe that you are a separate being existing in an external world, your idea of "mind" changes. Mind no longer means creative mind for you. Mind is now understood as a separate fragment of perceiving consciousness encased in a body. You no longer understand your experiences as the creative reflections of your ideas and beliefs. Instead, you believe that your experiences are caused by an external world that somehow impacts your mind. More precisely, other bodies somehow impact your own body—for instance, through emitting photons and sound waves—and then your own impacted body causes your "mind" to have sensations of the world. You believe that what you perceive and how you feel are determined, at least in large part, by an external world of bodies that is beyond your control.

That world beyond your control follows its own laws, such as the laws of physics and chemistry and biology. These laws describe how bodies interact with and cause changes in one another and how the past determines the present.

In this way of thinking about your life, you will believe that your mind is subject to your body. If your body is subject to all of the other bodies in the world and their causal laws, then your mind is also subject to those external things and laws. You will believe that what you experience now and how you feel are all somehow determined and limited by what is happening outside your mind—and most especially by what has already happened in the past.

Thus we see how the idea of separation can ultimately give rise to a whole way of experiencing yourself and the world. You no longer experience the world as a reflection of your thoughts but rather as an independent reality. You no longer experience your happiness and unhappiness as under your own control but rather as at the mercy of a world of external forces and powers. You no longer experience your mind as the creative center of your experience but rather as a limited and vulnerable fragment of consciousness that reacts to an external world. Basically your free creative mind has created the illusory experience that it is a victim.

I am not saying, however, that the whole world is just "in your head." What I am saying is that your whole *experience* of yourself-in-a-world is in your awareness. You can think of being-in-a-world as one possible kind of self-awareness—the kind of self-awareness that is in the form of a "you" character relating to "others" in an on-going interpretive narrative.

By definition, of course, the "world" and "others" are external to that "you" character in your awareness—that "you" with its own private perceiving consciousness encased in its own private body. But ultimately, the experience of *both* the "you" character *and* the "world" exist *in* your awareness. Or another way to express this is that the self-awareness of your mind exists, at least in this level of consciousness, *as* a relationship between a "you" and a "world." The whole of your mind is much more than the "you" character in that relationship.

We start our lives in this relational kind of self-awareness. But it is up to each of us individually to choose how we will think of our relationship with the "others."

If you identify completely with the "you" character, then you will tend to think of the world and others as "external" to you, and fundamentally separate and different from you. This way of thinking will be reflected as the experience of some degree of conflict and struggle, and all of your relationships will necessarily have an undercurrent of fear. All of this conflict and fear will be *within* your awareness. But you interpret it *as* a conflict between you and outside forces.

It is important to realize that "externality" is only a thought and an interpretation, and not a given fact or reality. But to say that the externality of the world is "only a thought and an interpretation" does not collapse our world to a tiny egocentric point and absolve us of relating to others. In fact, at the level of creative mind, we *are* our relationships. But it is only when we realize that separation and externality are only thoughts, that we are free, *for the first time,* to explore other possibilities of communication and compassion and love.

For some readers, this assertion that externality is only a thought may sound a bit extreme. It certainly seems that the externality of the world is simply a "fact" rather than a mere interpretation. "Reality," with all of its conflicts and threats and suffering, seems to exist "out there." It is simply a given, and that is why we perceive it that way. But we have only to look at our experience of dreaming at night to see that our minds can make up an entire world of experience. When we are dreaming, the world certainly seems to be external from the perspective of the dreamed character. And everyone in the dream agrees that this is so. But when you wake up, you realize "it was just a dream," meaning that there was nothing external to your awareness causing all of those sensations and perceptions of a world. I am not trying to convince you that the world is just a dream (although there is no way we could actually prove otherwise). What I am saying is that "externality" is just one possible interpretation of our experience. And it may be an interpretation that actually blocks our ability to be truly happy.

Remember that the whole purpose of this system of thought is to allow us to heal our perceptions of unhappiness and un-well-being, and to allow ourselves to experience more happiness and more well-being. I have found that when I think about myself and the world in terms of these seven principles, my experience shifts radically. There is a shift in both how I interpret what happens, and in what actually happens (insofar as these two can be distinguished). In every case it is a shift of healing—a shift of my perception from fear to love, from conflict to harmony, from sickness to health, from lack to greater abundance. This is not the result of my merely repeating the words of the principles, but rather actually living them and experiencing my life through them. This shift of perception happens every time I shift my belief system back to these principles. The more completely I am able to shift my mind, the more completely my perceptions are shifted.

Once again, your question may be: Will these seven principles work for *you*? When you shift your mind to these principles, will that cause a healing shift in *your* perceptions? The only way to find out is to actually live these principles, even if some of them may sound a bit strange to you at first. Are you already perfectly happy? If not, then try these ideas and see what happens.

Practicing the Principle of Creative Mind

Practice disengaging your attention from the objects of your awareness and becoming the awareness itself. Remember that awareness itself is not an object of awareness that you can focus on, not a "something" that you can hold in your mind. You can experience this openness only in the sense of self-awarely *being* the openness, which means becoming aware of yourself as this openness. You are not struggling against anything, or trying to repress anything. Simply let the objects of your awareness be what they are and shift your attention to the openness within which they come and go.

For this practice, find a quiet place where you will not be disturbed. Sit comfortably, close your eyes, and take three deep slow breaths to relax. Then open your eyes and read the next paragraph, and follow that part as best you can. Then read the next paragraph after that, and then close your eyes and follow that part. And so on until you have completed the exercise.

Start by disengaging your attention from anything you are seeing or hearing now. Become the openness in which these sights and sounds are coming and going.

Disengage your attention from all of the touch sensations you are aware of now. Become the openness.

Disengage your attention from the kinesthetic sensations of your own body and from any bodily sensations of health or sickness you are feeling now. Become the openness.

Disengage your attention from any emotions you are feeling now. Become the openness.

Disengage your attention from any thoughts that are in your mind. Again, you are not trying to hide or stop the thoughts. You are simply shifting your attention to self-awarely be the openness within which the thoughts are coming and going.

2 Look at your life from the perspective of *creative* mind. Think of your experiences as the result of your thoughts either allowing or distorting source's creative potential for ever-expanding well-being. Remember that this is not a matter of blame but rather of trying to understand your own co-creative role in your experience. How does this change how you respond to others and the world?

(And don't use this exercise to blame others for the problems you perceive in their lives. No one is intentionally making the experience of guilt or suffering in their lives. Focus on changing your own thoughts and taking responsibility for your own experience, and extend only compassion and love to others.)

3 When you experience any darkness in your life—any lack of love or joy or well-being—ask yourself, "How can I *extend* more light now?" Discover for yourself how extending something different from yourself changes what you receive.

PRINCIPLE THREE
ALLOWING HAPPINESS

*You can choose to think thoughts
that allow your awareness to
more fully and clearly manifest the
truth of happiness and well-being in
your experience, rather than thoughts that
restrict your awareness. When you allow
happiness in your own experience, you
also help others to more fully realize
that possibility for themselves.*

Most of us find ourselves already within a belief system that tells us that we can only have a limited amount of happiness and that this happiness is largely dependent on external conditions. Furthermore, we believe that to achieve and maintain this limited happiness, we have to somehow "do it right." This "doing it right" can take the form of religious rules we must obey, or a work ethic we must adhere to, or even a New Age regimen of positive affirmations and visualizations we must follow. We have been taught that we have to somehow earn or make our happiness by doing the right things in the right way. You have to do enough and keep doing enough.

This chapter offers another alternative—the possibility of becoming happier through struggling less. This doesn't mean apathy or passivity. It's more like *the joyful active allowing of happiness.*

Joyful Active Allowing

You can think of happiness as either something that has to be earned or attained through effort, or as the natural state of your being that has simply to be allowed. You can think of your journey to the light as either a struggle against the forces of darkness, or as a joyful process of allowing yourself to become and be who you already truly are.

Many people tend to believe that we live in a hard world and that we can achieve happiness only through hard work, struggle and self-sacrifice. They think it is utterly unrealistic to aspire to perfect happiness and to expect to be happy all of the time. Some religions even teach that you start off as a "miserable sinner." Before you can be happy, you have to somehow "atone" for your guilt, your inherent badness. And whatever small degree of happiness is possible can be attained only by overcoming your inherent nature, only by defeating yourself.

Plus, you have to be very guarded about any happiness you might feel, because it could be taken away at any moment. From this perspective, there is always a hostile Nature or a jealous God just waiting to take you down a notch. So you have to "knock on wood" every time you speak of your good fortune, so that an unfriendly universe won't snatch it away from you.

This whole belief system is reflected in many of the self-help books and seminars available today, which seem to teach that becoming happy and staying happy is a lot of work. You have to learn the "right" techniques, and you have to do them the "right" way, and you have to do them diligently and constantly. Often you simply have to take it on faith that the techniques a given teacher is promoting are the "right" ones.

But even if you are lucky enough to choose the right techniques, and you are able to do them in just the right way, and you are diligent and persistent, success and happiness might still elude you. Most of these techniques are ways of changing or manipulating the world and other people in order to create circumstances that are favorable for you. And *then* you can be happy, at least for as long as you continue to diligently do the right things in the right way. The problem, however, is that other people are also using those techniques to change the world and create favorable circumstance for themselves (which might not always be the most favorable circumstances for *your* happiness). And, sometimes, they are better at the whole process than you. They either have better techniques, or they do them better, or they are more tirelessly consistent than you. Sometimes it seems that some people just have personalities that are better suited to imposing their will on the world—they are more outgoing, more self-confident and just better at manipulating others. The teachers of such seminars often seem to have this kind of personality. And perhaps some people are just luckier than you, or have better karma.

So we go from one teacher to the next, always looking for better techniques, or at least techniques more suited to our own values and personalities. But even when we succeed—temporarily creating more success, more abundance, more happiness in our lives—it can seem like a lot of work and create stress. You can't quit doing your techniques for a moment. And you have to be on the lookout for even better techniques. Plus you always have to keep your guard up against everyone else doing their techniques. You have to make sure that you're making the world be the way that you want it to be rather than letting them make it their way. On top of that, even when you do all this work, you only succeed sometimes.

But there is another possibility. Our first two principles give us a good foundation for an alternative approach to happiness: the belief that happiness is natural. Since the only real power in the universe is the potential for well-being, happiness is simply the natural and unrestricted expression of that power in your life that occurs when you are allowing your mind to manifest source fully and clearly.

Seen in this light, *happiness is your higher purpose*. You don't have to struggle against and overcome anything, you don't have to earn anything or atone for anything—you simply have to accept and fulfill your own truth, your own nature. Happiness is simply the emotional reflection of you allowing yourself to be yourself. *Happiness is the expression of your alignment with your own truth.*

You might ask, which approach is the "right" one? I'm not sure that there is an answer to this question. But if I believe that happiness can be attained or earned only through constant struggle, only through an on-going uncertain effort to manipulate the world, then I will experience my life in that way. I will work and struggle and sacrifice, and my efforts will sometimes be rewarded with success and sometimes not. If I believe that we actively allow happiness through a joyful alignment with our deeper truth, then I will have a very different kind of life experience. But what exactly is involved in this active allowing?

How to Allow Happiness

As an extension of creative source, your mind is creative. Your experience is the co-creation resulting from the interaction of your thoughts (beliefs, desires, focus of attention) and the pure positive energy of source. Your thoughts provide the form, and source provides the power and the content. "Your thoughts" include all of your thoughts, both conscious and subconscious, both personal and those you share with others.

As we saw in principle two, there are basically two kinds of thoughts: source-like thoughts and un-source-like thoughts. Source-like thoughts are thoughts of one power, of well-being, of love and happiness and abundance in every area of life.

Un-source-like thoughts include thoughts about two powers, thoughts about the restriction or limitation of well-being, and thoughts about un-well-being, unworthiness and lack. Source-like thoughts are always accompanied by feelings of peace and happiness. Un-source-like thoughts are always accompanied by an undercurrent of unease, and feelings of fear, anxiety, anger or dread.

Source-like thoughts are *revealing* thoughts. They *allow* your mind to clearly and unhiddenly express the infinite creative potential for well-being in your experience—to creatively express source-power as experiences of joy, of love, of peace, of health, of abundance, of well-being.

Un-source-like thoughts are *concealing* thoughts. They *restrict* your mind from fully manifesting the infinite creative potential for well-being in your experience. Your experience of restricted or limited well-being always takes the form of seemingly real experiences of un-well-being—experiences of unhappiness, lack and sickness; experiences of a fearful and threatening world.

It is important to note that "un-source-like thoughts" do not necessarily mean thoughts of pure badness or pure evil, if such thoughts are possible at all. Un-source-like thoughts are typically thoughts about limitation and lack, about a *mixture* of good and bad. That is to say that un-source-like thoughts are *dualistic* thoughts. This mixture kind of thinking will be creatively expressed as a mixture kind of life experience—a mixture of happiness and unhappiness, of good and bad, of limited well-being and limited un-well-being. And as we have seen above, mixture or two-power thinking is always, implicitly or explicitly, a denial of the principle of one power.

The first page of the book *A Course in Miracles* says, "The course does not aim at teaching the meaning of love, for that is beyond what can be taught. It does aim, however, at removing the blocks to the awareness of love's presence, which is your natural inheritance." Similarly, we could say that the way to happiness is the undoing of your blocks to your awareness of source, to your awareness of your own true nature. Being happy is a matter of choosing the thoughts and the beliefs and the focus of attention that most fully *allow* your mind to express the nature of source in and as your own life experience.

This means choosing to *not* think those thoughts or dwell on those things that restrict your mind from fully expressing source in your experience. Being unhappy is always a reflection that you are actively restricting your own innate happiness, limiting your own innate potential to co-create joy. Unhappiness doesn't happen "to" you—it is always a matter of you *making* yourself unhappy. When you release your attention from those thoughts that are unhappy thoughts for you, you allow your nature as a creative expression of well-being to more fully express itself.

Allowing your own happiness by choosing to think only thoughts of love and joy is not a selfish and egocentric enterprise. In a two-power belief system, you have to focus on both good and evil. It would be foolish, naive, unrealistic and dangerous to ignore the bad in the world. It would even be irresponsible, since a "good person" is morally obligated to hate evil. In fact, fighting against evil is viewed as one way we can help others.

From the perspective of one power, however, "fighting evil" would be a very irresponsible way of being. Fearfully focusing your attention on the seemingly "bad" things of life would be an implicit affirmation of two powers. It would blind you to the very possibility of experiencing perfect joy and well-being. You don't have to "fight evil" in order to be good. You can simply choose to love. You can offer kindness and support, without reacting to the appearances of guilt or suffering. You can compassionately respond to others' needs, and you can take whatever actions you believe are necessary, without feeling afraid, angry, upset or unpeaceful.

Your negative emotional reaction to the apparent negativity in the world will only reinforce others' beliefs in the reality of a second power. Even if you provide temporary comfort or solace for another, if you do it from an unhappy or fearful state of mind, you will have effectively made his own mental prison of suffering seem more real and impenetrable. If, however, you can hold the vision of the other's creative freedom, of his potential to co-create a life experience of perfect well-being, then you are able to practice compassion without pity or fear or anger. And that vision may well be the most healing and valuable thing you can share with another.

To summarize this section in the simplest terms, you allow happiness when you think happy thoughts. You disallow happiness when you think unhappy thoughts. To say this a little more precisely, when you choose to think happy thoughts, you allow your mind to be open to possibilities of feeling happiness and having happy experiences. When you think unhappy thoughts, you restrict your mind's ability to realize possibilities of happy feelings and experiences. And your allowing or restricting thoughts tend to have the same influence on others' minds. When you consciously choose happy thoughts, everyone benefits.

Happiness Is Always Available Within

The good news is that you don't need to control or change your circumstances in order to be happy. The effort to control others and the world is uncertain at best, and sometimes even feels manipulative and wrong. No, what you have to change is simply your own mind—your thoughts and beliefs, your focus of attention, your state of mind. And that is in your control, because you can always shift your attention to a happier thought. The only time it seems difficult to do this is when you are attached to an unhappy thought. But since you have to actively maintain that attachment, you always have the choice of stopping.

This means that *happiness is always available in every now*, regardless of the apparent circumstances of your life. Your happiness is literally an inside job.

From this perspective, your happiness is never a matter of somehow battling or overcoming external circumstances and events. In fact, it is precisely the belief that your happiness is somehow dependent on external persons and conditions that makes you unhappy. You define yourself as a victim who is at the mercy of things and forces that are outside your mind, and then you fearfully try to control those forces. Even when you temporarily succeed and get what you want, you are still fearful, because it may change or be taken away from you by another. If the seeming cause of your happiness is another person, she might change her mind, or he might die. So there is never any complete happiness, since you are always either fearfully trying to make the outside world be a certain way, fearfully trying to keep it a certain way, fearfully trying to get something or fearfully trying to avoid something. In this belief system, fear is the one constant underlying everything you do and feel.

The belief that happiness comes from outside is the cause of every experience of unhappiness—the cause of every feeling of being unfairly treated, every feeling of fear or anger. The belief that I am separate or cut off from the source of my happiness will always generate a life experience of fear and unhappiness. Trying to find happiness, either by desperately pursuing or desperately running away from the things of the world, will never work, not in any real or abiding sense. Not only will it not work, but the very attempt to do this will actually result in experiences of unhappiness.

Happiness comes from within. One helpful way to think about this is that there is *a "place" in your mind,* a dimension of consciousness, a state of awareness where happiness is *always* available. Being happy is a matter of shifting your focus of attention to that place in your mind. It is not a matter of changing the things and circumstances that you experience, but rather of changing the state of mind from which you experience them. The experience of happiness, peace of mind, unconditional love and well-being is always available, available in every now—not merely sometime later after you have changed things in your life, but *now*, right where you are.

To shift into this place or dimension of peace within your own mind necessarily involves a kind of *acceptance* of how things are. If you are caught up in fear or anger or worry about the world, in any judgments or grievances about the world—in any attachment to the world being a certain way—then you are actively keeping yourself from that place of perfect peace in your mind.

The concern here, of course, is that such acceptance would become mere passivity, and would cause you to fail in your responsibility to "do the right thing." Sometimes it seems that fear or anger is what alerts you to the need for action. But they are never good guides for truly helpful action. As we noted earlier, what you really offer to another in any interaction is your state of mind, the kind of consciousness from which your words and actions are proceeding. Your state of mind of perfect peace, your vision of the underlying truth of goodness, is the most healing thing you can offer anyone in any situation, regardless of what you do or don't do.

Acceptance is not a substitute for action, nor is it an excuse not to act. It is rather the fundamental ground from which all truly helpful action flows. Acceptance does not mean passivity or ignoring others' calls for help and support. What it means is simply letting appearances be what they are. You shift into that deeper place of mind of perfect peace and then let the most healing words or actions flow from that place.

The Now of Infinite Possibility

When *you choose* to believe that your experience of the world is caused by external realities following their own causal laws, then what you believe you can experience next is limited to a relatively small spectrum of possibilities. You will believe that the past determines, at least for the most part, the present and the future. You will believe that your own range of possible choices, what you can think or feel or do or be, is limited by your own personal history and by the "objective" circumstances of your life. For instance, you might tell yourself the story that "I can't be completely loving and happy now because I was scarred by an abusive childhood." Or, "I can't ever be well again because I have been diagnosed with an incurable disease." And since your experiences are the reflections of your thoughts, these limiting beliefs will be reflected as limitations in your experience.

When you are lost in the dream of being a small vulnerable mind at the mercy of an external world, your experiences will confirm your belief that what happens to you in your life is largely beyond your control. From that perspective, this whole discussion about "choice" will seem to be naïve and unrealistic. You will think that the externality of the material world with its causal laws of space and time is simply "given," is simply the objective reality of life.

But there is another possible alternative. You could choose to believe in infinite possibility. Your belief in limited possibility is simply the denial of infinite possibility. Choosing to believe in infinite possibility is just the undoing of your belief in limited possibility, the undoing of your denial of infinite possibility.

You can choose to believe that you are creative mind, a creative expression of the infinite creative source of all life. You can choose to believe that your experiences—your interpreted, meaningful experiences of yourself and the world—are reflections of your thoughts and beliefs. Your choice to believe in *creative* mind is the choice to believe in a *now of infinite possibility*—in particular, the infinite possibility of healing and well-being. The infinite eternal creative power of source is not determined or limited by the world or the past. That is what is meant by "infinite" and "eternal."

The belief in limited possibility is a self-imposed limitation that will effectively restrict what you can perceive and how you can interpret it. As you begin to shift your belief to a now of infinite possibility, you make yourself more open to unexpected, serendipitous, and even seemingly impossible or miraculous experiences.

You will open your awareness to the previously unknown and unimagined—perhaps even to the previously unimaginable.

From the perspective of the now of infinite possibility, what you can do next, what can happen next in your life, what healing is possible in your life or the lives of others, what ever-expanding possibilities of well-being are possible—none of this is pre-determined. The belief in a now of infinite possibility is the belief that healing is always possible, regardless of the past. Not only is it possible, but it can even be instantaneous and can transcend the seemingly immutable causal laws of the world.

The choice to believe in a now of infinite possibility is the choice to believe that you, in your truth, are *free of the past*—at least in terms of the well-being and healing you can experience now. To say that source is *eternally* creative means that creation—including the creation of you—is happening anew in every moment, and it is being driven by the *infinite* (i.e., *unlimited*) power of love. And beyond love, there is nothing.

The only way you can discover for yourself that your belief choice in limited possibilities is indeed *just a belief choice* is from the perspective of an alternative belief choice. And it is only in *living* an alternative belief choice that you can discover its truth for *you*, that you can discover whether or not it opens *you* to a deeper and richer life experience. What would happen to your life experience if you believed in a now of infinite possibility? Find out.

Practicing the Principle of
Allowing Happiness

1 Sit now and consider anything in your life you currently feel unhappy about. Ask yourself, "How am *I making* myself unhappy now? What unhappy thoughts am I choosing to think now?" Notice any reasons or justifications that you give yourself for continuing to remain unhappy now. Ask yourself what you are afraid might happen if you allowed yourself to be completely happy now. What would happen if you, just for a moment, let go of every thought of why you must or should be unhappy now?

In the course of your day-to-day life when you find yourself feeling unhappy in any way, ask yourself these same questions.

2 This is a meditation for your peace of mind. Set aside a quiet time without distractions. Imagine that there is an ever-present place in your mind where you feel only perfect peace, perfect love and perfect joy. That place is already and eternally within your mind. Start to shift your attention to that inner place. Begin by letting go of, or disengaging your attention from, any thoughts and sensations that are incompatible with that place—any unpeaceful or unloving or unhappy thoughts. Focus only on thoughts that reflect love and joy. Let yourself gently settle into that inner place of perfect peace, and simply be there.

Repeat this practice whenever you can. As you become more and more familiar with how to get to that place of inner peace, you will be able to move there quickly when you are faced with "challenges" in your daily life.

3   This is a meditation for freedom. Set aside a quiet time without distractions. Consider the infinite possibility of this now-moment. Let go of every thought that this now is somehow limited or determined by the past. Ask yourself, "How would now look to me if I had no limiting thoughts about my age or my personal history?" This is not a matter of denying your age or your personal history but rather of letting go of every thought that they limit your possibilities for healing and happiness now. Let go of every thought that you have been somehow wounded or scarred by your past in a way that limits your possibilities for experiencing love and joy now. Does this change how you see yourself now? Does it change how you think about your future now? Does it change how you feel now?

This practice can also be helpful especially when you are feeling that your possibilities for happiness or healing or well-being are somehow limited by the past. What new possibilities come to light when you let go of your *thoughts* about those limits?

You can also meditate on the now of infinite possibility with respect to "future nows." This can be especially helpful when you are faced with what seems to be a difficult decision. Often the feeling of difficulty comes from the fearful thought that what you choose may limit your future possibilities. Remind yourself that every now carries infinite possibility. Remind yourself that the creative power of source is never limited by what has gone before. Source's eternal creative power is infinite in every now. When you are no longer fearful about the future, how does that change your choices now?

PRINCIPLE FOUR
JOYFUL
MANIFESTATION

You are an individual
expression of the infinite eternal
creative potential for well-being.
Your desires are the exuberant
expression of your creative nature.
Joyful thoughts allow you to
experience the manifestation of
the truth of your desires.

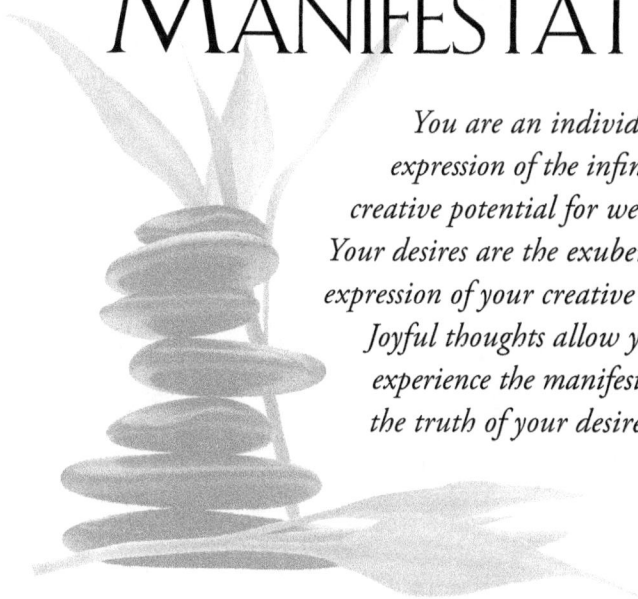

Desire and manifestation: This is clearly one of the most popular topics in the self-help and happiness literature today. The prevailing idea is that we will be really happy when all of our current desires are manifested—when we become and have everything we want. So the real key to happiness is to figure out how to manifest our desires—how to "make" our dreams come true.

Obviously the approach of these seven principles is that happiness comes from within and is available in every moment. It is not dependent on "manifesting" any particular thing or condition at all. But we do in fact have desires. What role do desires play in this way of thinking about the world? If we desire certain things in our lives such as health, material abundance and joyful relationships, aren't we falling into the trap of making our happiness dependent on external circumstances? And isn't that the primary cause of unhappiness? Is the answer to simply get rid of all desires? That certainly doesn't seem very desirable.

Desires do seem to be a natural part of our human existence. Without any conscious or deliberate effort on our part, we find ourselves desiring things and conditions and situations and relationships in our lives. Sometimes this whole process of desiring seems to add to the joy of life. Other times it seems that our desires end up bringing us anxiety, frustration, disappointment and unhappiness.

When we consider what various traditions and teachers have said about desire, we find contradictory opinions. Some traditions claim that desires are the ultimate cause of all unhappiness, and that we should work to extinguish all our desires and simply be. Other approaches claim that the fulfillment of our desires is the way to happiness, and they teach us practices and techniques to make our dreams come true. Many people find themselves somewhere in the middle. On the one hand, they do have desires, and they want worldly things and conditions. On the other hand, they feel that such wanting is somehow materialistic and unspiritual, and so they feel vaguely uneasy about wholeheartedly pursuing their desires.

In sorting this out for ourselves, it is important to realize that it may not be desire itself that is the problem, but rather how we define and understand desire, and how we think about and understand the process of realizing or manifesting our desires. Our thoughts about the whole cycle of desiring and manifestation are what determine whether it is a joyful co-creative process in our lives or a process that is desperate, fearful and unfulfilling.

Desires can be a wonderful part of our lives and allow us to deeply experience and fulfill our creative nature. But for desires to play such a positive role in our lives, without at the same time bringing disappointment and despair, we must take care about how we understand desire and how we understand ourselves. The positive or negative effect that desires have on our lives is ultimately only a reflection of our own level of self-awareness.

Happiness-based Desires

Desires are thoughts of conditions or circumstances that you would like to come to pass in your life—those conditions and circumstances that would best symbolize well-being for you. Desires are a natural expression of your creative mind. They are simply one way that your creative mind expresses its truth as a be-ing of the infinite eternal creative potential for ever-expanding well-being. Your creative mind expresses its infinite creative potential for ever-expanding well-being by imagining the conditions and circumstances that would best symbolize expanded well-being for it, and then translating those desires into experiences.

The manifestation of your desires is one expression of the co-creative partnership between the pure positive energy of source and your creative mind. The infinite creative potential for ever-expanding well-being is your truth, your essence. Your desires can give this creative source potential the specific forms that it uses to fulfill or realize its creativity in and as your experience. You *are* a be-ing of the realizing of source. And this process of realizing source *is* the process of realizing your own truth.

But it often seems that not all of our desires are manifested. We don't always get what we want. Sometimes, we seem to get exactly what we don't want. And sometimes when we get exactly what we have been wishing for, it doesn't make us happy at all. If the whole process of desire and manifestation is natural and spontaneous, why does it seem to be so hit and miss? How can we more consistently and happily manifest what we truly desire? Here, "what we truly desire" means the underlying truth of our desires: the experience or the manifestation of ever-expanding well-being.

It is important to distinguish between a fear-based desire and a happiness-based desire. These two kinds of desires arise out of two different kinds of self-definition and self-awareness.

A fear-based desire is based on a belief in lack. To desire something fearfully is to believe that you *need* it. This implies that you define yourself as lacking. You believe that you lack what you need to be happy and fulfilled, and that something external is necessary for your happiness. You believe that getting or achieving this thing will "make" you happy. And conversely, you believe that getting or having certain other things will make you unhappy.

Need- or fear-based desires include all of our desperate cravings, such as the desperate cravings for fame or money or power or pleasure. The key word here is "desperate," since fame and money and power and pleasure are not problems in themselves, nor is there anything inherently wrong with our desires for such things.

A need- or fear-based desire creates unhappiness in your life. It is an implicit affirmation that you are unhappy and lacking now. When you believe that you are lacking and unhappy now, that thought will be reflected as experiences of lack and unhappiness. The belief in the inherent limitedness of yourself or the world will be reflected as experiences of restricted well-being in your life—that is to say, experiences of un-well-being. Thus when you believe that you are needy and lacking now, that belief is making you feel unhappy in the present. It is an un-source-like thought that is being emotionally reflected as unhappiness. It is also laying the foundation for future unhappy experiences, since your belief in your neediness will be creatively expressed as further experiences of lack.

Furthermore, to believe that something outside your mind is necessary for your happiness is necessarily a fearful state of mind. After all, you might not get it, or you might get its opposite. And you know that even if you do get it, you may (or even definitely will) eventually lose it. These fearful thoughts that are implicit in a need- or fear-based desire will be creatively translated by mind into the experience of some degree of un-well-being in your life. As we said earlier, your belief that your happiness is dependent on external circumstances is the cause of your experience of unhappiness.

The alternative to a fear-based desire is a happiness-based desire. The starting point for a happiness-based desire is the belief that you are already complete now. You start in and from that place in your own mind of perfect happiness. You know you are a joyful co-creator of joyful experiences. In your creative exuberance, you allow your creative desires to rise up from within, and you joyfully hold them in your awareness in the absolute belief that the loving source of all life will creatively translate them into experience. After all, there is *only* the infinite creative potential for well-being, the flow toward ever-expanding goodness. This is the only truth, the only cause, the only power. In complete faith, you joyfully anticipate and await the manifestation of your desires, either in the particular form that you have envisioned, or in an even better form that you cannot yet imagine.

And yet—and this is of the utmost importance—there is nothing at stake for you in whether or not your desires are manifested, because you *know* that you already have and are everything you need for perfect happiness. This is the delicate balance of a happiness-based desire—a balance of joyfully wanting something with all your heart, and at the same time a sense of perfect equanimity. Both the desire itself and its manifestation are *expressions* of your happiness, rather than attempts to somehow get or achieve happiness. They are the exuberant creative expressions of your overflowing abundance, rather than a desperate grasping for something you think you lack.

Your mind naturally and spontaneously generates desires in its own playful creativity. Source, in its infinite loving benevolence, naturally and spontaneously provides the creative energy that manifests these desires as experiences. The creative potential of source *is* the fulfilling of the forms of creative mind, and the desires of creative mind *are* the informing and realizing of the creative potential of source. Your experience is the result of this co-creative partnership of the pure positive energy of source in conjunction with the thoughts and desires of your creative mind.

Downstream and Upstream Thoughts

This whole creative process is mediated by your thoughts and beliefs. Earlier we said that we can distinguish between two kinds of thoughts: source-like thoughts and un-source-like thoughts. We said that source-like thoughts are thoughts about one power, about well-being, about love and happiness and abundance in every area of life. Un-source-like thoughts include thoughts about two powers, thoughts about the restriction or limitation of well-being, thoughts about un-well-being and thoughts about unworthiness.

Source-like thoughts can be characterized as *allowing* thoughts or *revealing* thoughts. They allow your mind to *unhiddenly manifest* source energy as the experience of ever-expanding well-being.

We can think of source as an eternal flow toward ever-expanding goodness. And this thrust or flow is the truth of every moment—an infinite creative potential for well-being, waiting to be given form. In terms of the metaphor of the eternal "flow," source-like or allowing thoughts would be "downstream" thoughts. Downstream thoughts are thoughts that allow your mind to manifest the flow toward ever-expanding well-being as experiences of ever-expanding well-being. (I am indebted to Jerry and Esther Hicks and Abraham for this wonderful metaphor of downstream and upstream thoughts. I am developing this metaphor somewhat differently from them, although I do think it is consistent with their ideas.)

Un-source-like thoughts, on the other hand, can be characterized as *restricting* thoughts or *concealing* thoughts. They restrict your mind from fully expressing and experiencing the creative potential for ever-expanding well-being. Thus, they give rise to un-source-like experiences (victimhood, evil, suffering, sickness, lack, fear, etc.) that conceal the true nature of source and the true nature of your own being. In terms of the metaphor of the eternal "flow," un-source-like or restricting thoughts would be "upstream" thoughts—thoughts that go against the flow toward ever-expanding well-being and effectively hide its nature beneath illusory experiences of un-well-being.

Feelings are the emotional reflections of thoughts. You can know which kind of thoughts you are thinking by how you feel. Source-like or allowing thoughts feel good. Un-source-like or restricting thoughts feel bad. In other words, downstream thoughts that allow your true desires to be realized also allow you to feel happy while you are thinking them. Upstream thoughts that restrict the realization of your dreams also restrict your happiness while you are thinking them.

Downstream thoughts are accompanied by a sense of ease. Upstream thoughts tend to be accompanied by a sense of struggle. This does not mean, however, that going downstream involves no effort. But it is a joyful effort that arises from and expresses a happy state of mind. There is no sense of struggling against anything you don't want—you are simply joyfully co-creating what you do want.

Everything you want is downstream. Downstream thoughts allow you to feel happy now, and they allow you to have future experiences of ever-expanding well-being.

Nothing that you want is upstream. Upstream thoughts not only make you feel unhappy now, but also have a restrictive effect on the manifestation of all of your desires.

The real issue is not the form of a particular desire but rather the level of consciousness of the desirer. For your heart's desires to fully manifest as happy experiences, you must create and hold and live those desires from a state of mind of happiness. The critical element is not so much what you desire and what you manifest, but rather the quality of the desiring and manifesting process itself. Once again, your happy experiences do not cause you to be happy. Your happy experiences are the creative manifestation of your happy state of mind and your happy thoughts.

Since the truth of everyone is *creative* mind, *my* fulfillment of *my* desires cannot take anything away from *you*—cannot limit *your* fulfillment of *your* desires, and cannot restrict *your* experience of well-being. That fear is based on the belief that there is an external world of limited resources, and that one person's gain is always another's loss. But if each person's life experience is the co-creative result of the partnership of the *infinite* creative potential of source combined with his own desires, then no one can really deprive another in any way.

But if we say that each person is responsible for his own experience of well-being, isn't there the danger we will become selfish and uncaring? Instead of reaching out in compassion and support to those who we see as poor or sick or abused, wouldn't we simply blame the "victims" for their suffering?

Because we are all expressions of the same one power, we share a common truth and essence. One way this sharing expresses itself is as your innate compassion for others. At the deepest level, they, like you, are individualized expressions of creative mind. In other words, all of the individualized selves are expressions of the one Self shared by all. This means that all of the other beings you encounter are your other selves. So when you see another lost in his self-created illusion of suffering, you spontaneously feel a desire to somehow offer help and healing to him.

Ultimately, of course, he will have to change his own thoughts and beliefs in order to create real change in his life. Your part in helping him is to somehow awaken him to his own role in the co-creation of his experience. Often the intermediate steps to this awakening involve reducing the fear in his life that is blinding him to his true nature. You may reduce the fear in his life by offering emotional support or material assistance. But for this offering to be truly helpful, it must arise out of *your vision* of his underlying wholeness and completeness.

In this process, blaming is never helpful. True compassion never attacks. Adding guilt to another's experience of suffering only compounds his belief in limitation and vulnerability. Your role is to help him awaken from his nightmare not to drive him further into it. There is no place for any negative judgments in this healing process—no place for any judgments of evil or lack or blame. There is only your vision of the other's truth of absolute worth, absolute wholeness, absolute abundance and absolute creative freedom.

An essential part of expressing your compassion for others is actually living a happy life yourself and manifesting your own dreams and desires. Your own happiness serves as an inspiration to help them realize their own creative potential for happiness.

Interrupting Negative Emotional Habits

One of the greatest obstacles to manifesting what we truly desire is "what is"—i.e., what we are currently experiencing as the seemingly real absence of what we want or the seemingly real presence of what we don't want. While we try to focus our attention on what we want, we are at the same time thinking about currently having or being what we don't want. Since we are thinking about both what we want and what we don't want, this will be creatively translated into further experiences of both what we want and what we don't want.

As creative mind, you are continually engaged in the co-creation of your life experience. The power for this on-going co-creation comes from source, which is perfect love, the infinite creative potential for well-being. Your co-creative role is to give specific form to source's pure positive energy; to shape the infinite potential for well-being with the thoughts and desires that arise in your individual creative mind. Your thoughts either allow your mind to clearly manifest this power as happy experiences of well-being, or to restrict it so that you experience some degree of lack and suffering.

You will know what kind of thoughts you are thinking in two ways. First, by how you feel: you feel good when you are thinking allowing thoughts, and you feel bad when you are thinking restricting thoughts. Second, by what is manifesting in your experience: your experience reveals to you how much of the infinite well-being of life you have been willing to allow into your experience. As Arnold Patent said in a recorded lecture, "Look around you. This is as good as you can stand it."

Of course, no one deliberately sets out to limit the expression of well-being in her experience; no one consciously and deliberately tries to make experiences of sickness or suffering or lack, experiences of hostile and fearful things and events. But to whatever degree you believe in separation, in two powers, in an external world that victimizes you, you will necessarily make a life experience of fear and lack.

"What is" becomes an obstacle in your mind only when you think of it as an external reality in and of itself, having an independent power to determine what you experience and how you feel. It is this *interpretation* of "what is" that makes it a mental prison—a thought-prison made by the mind that limits your possible awareness, limits what you believe you can think and feel and do and experience. Mind has imprisoned itself by imagining that it is not free.

One way we imprison ourselves is through our emotional addictions that determine how we think about and how we look at the world. If you are emotionally addicted to depression, for instance, you will tend to focus on the thoughts and images and memories and anticipations that you find depressing—the ones that you think "make" you depressed. You will tend to look for things in the world that are depressing, and tend to interpret situations and relationships in terms of their potentially depressing qualities.

From the perspective of separation consciousness, you will believe that all of your patterns of unhappiness are caused by an unhappy world—a world that is depressing or frustrating or overwhelming or unjust; a world that provokes anger or fear or hatred; a world that scars and wounds us as we move through it. You don't necessarily believe that the world is all bad or negative. But you will tend to believe that there are negative elements in the very fabric of reality itself—that life in and of itself is to some extent depressing or frustrating.

Unless you are completely happy all of the time (in which case you would probably not be reading this book), you have some habits of negative thoughts and feelings. That is simply your starting point. Often we don't seem to deliberately choose our thoughts and feelings—we simply find ourselves in the midst of already thinking and feeling them. The real question is whether you *choose to indulge* in such thoughts and feelings once you are aware of them. The more you think about things that you feel unhappy about, or focus on aspects of the world that you feel fearful or angry or depressed about, the more you will reinforce your own negative emotional addictions.

As long as you are lost in the incessant chatter of your habitual thoughts, your habits are thinking for you. Thus your habits, rather than your own true desires, are giving rise to your experience. But you are not your habits and addictions. You are creative mind. In your truth you are the creative awareness within which that habitual "you," with its habits and addictions, exists. You can disengage from your identification with the habitual you and shift your focus to the openness itself.

When you make this shift of awareness, you are free to interrupt those patterns and addictions. You can choose to re-interpret an unhappy experience in a happier way. You can choose to think about or remember something that is happy for you. You can choose to shift your focus of attention to something that gives you joy. Every time you make that choice, every time you interrupt a negative pattern of thought and emotion, you weaken it. It becomes less compelling, and the next time it occurs it is easier to interrupt and disengage from. And gradually you begin to establish more positive patterns of thought and emotion.

Your experience is the reflection of the totality of your thoughts. You cannot co-create or manifest a life experience of perfect happiness from within a state of mind of habitual unhappiness. The more your thoughts are positive and focused on what you want and what you like, the more your experience will be in alignment with the nature of source itself. The happier thoughts you choose to think moment by moment will be reflected as happier experiences.

The more you realize that you are *creative* mind and that you are *free* to create and choose the thoughts that will be reflected as your experiences, the more you will be free from the seeming tyranny of "what is." You will no longer see it as an objective reality that must somehow be handled or dealt with. You will free yourself from the imagined need to battle and overcome things in the world. You will realize that thinking about and fighting against what you don't want will only tend to manifest more of it in your experience.

As free creative mind, you can choose what you think and what you focus on, and your experiences will reflect those choices. You are free to change your thoughts and beliefs *before* your experience changes. You are free to focus on what you want and simply not think one way or the other about what you don't want. In your own awareness you become the *process of co-creating* your experiences rather than some being that is defined and constrained by them. This is simply an extension of the first principle of one power. As creative mind, you do not have to react to or battle against a second power, because there is no second power.

The presence of what you don't want in your experience is never a reason to be unhappy or afraid. It is a reminder to think different thoughts, to believe different beliefs, to re-focus your attention on what you want. At any given moment, the question you want to ask yourself is, "What form do I want to give to the eternal infinite flow toward ever-expanding goodness *now?*" Not, "What form did I give it in the past that is now present as my current manifested experience?" but "What form do I want to give it *now?*" "What is" exists for you only as a friendly guide on your eternal creative journey. Experiencing what you don't want is simply an opportunity to refine and clarify your desires. In the *freedom of your creativity,* you can choose to focus *only* on what you want, on what gives you joy.

True Self-Awareness and True Desires

Earlier we distinguished between your awareness and what you typically think of as "you"—your personality, your personal history, your ego, your habits of thought and emotion, and all of the traits and qualities that define that you. We emphasized that this "you" is only one object of your awareness, one possible interpreted thought *within* your awareness. This "you" is not your creative mind. It is only one expression or one creation of your creative mind, one of the thoughts and experiences created by and existing in the openness.

At the deepest level, you are mind or awareness. But when you identify with the individual personality "you," you become a character in a story that your mind is making up. What you can think or feel or choose next is determined by that character's habits, tendencies and past history. You are like a character in a work of fiction, completely defined and bound by the narrative of the story. And so within the whole of your awareness, you experience yourself as that limited character rather than as the creative awareness of that character.

Your creative mind's thoughts and beliefs act with the infinite creative potential for well-being to co-create your life experience. Said in another way, the source energy of well-being actualizes itself through the specific forms of your thoughts and beliefs, and this actualization *is* your life experience. Your actual life experience is the co-creative result of the net meaning of *all* your thoughts, both conscious and subconscious. Depending on the kinds of thoughts you think, your experience may be a relatively clear and unhidden actualization of source's potential for well-being, or a partial and distorted manifestation.

When you identify with the personality "you"—a bundle of routines and tendencies and defined by its personal history—then all of your deliberate creative efforts will take place within that limited context of habitual thoughts and feelings. Your affirmation of a new car, for instance, may take place in the overall context of your habitual beliefs about scarcity and limitation, your habitual thoughts of conflict and struggle, your habitual beliefs about whether you are deserving or worthy enough, your habitual beliefs about the causal laws of external reality that limit what is possible in any given moment.

As a result, you may not always manifest or realize your conscious desires, if they are being restricted or disallowed by your subconscious limiting beliefs. And even if you do get what you think you want—for instance, the new car you have been affirming—you may find that the overall quality of your life experience is basically unchanged, since the quality of your life experience will be a reflection of the net quality of all of your beliefs. Based on this, some people will jump to the conclusion that either the idea of "you co-create your own reality" is untrue and doesn't work, or even if it does work, it doesn't really make any difference anyway.

True creative freedom takes place only at the level of mind or awareness—that level of pure awareness that both creates thoughts and experiences, and is the openness within which the thoughts and experiences exist for us. To fully realize your birthright as a co-creator of your experience, you need to shift your awareness to that deeper level of mind, to that dimension of consciousness. You need to shift your focus of attention from the thoughts and objects of awareness to the openness in which they come and go. Only from that kind of awareness can you be fully aware of your thoughts and freely choose which to give your attention to.

The only way to truly take over your full and free creative role in your own life experience is to somehow disengage yourself from your habitual identification with that "you" character. You have to shift to a level or dimension of awareness that is not defined or determined by your body, your personality, your habits of thought and feeling, and your personal history. This is the kind of awareness that mystics sometimes refer to as "the observer" or "the witness."

There is no shortcut to this level of consciousness. Since it is a matter of disengaging from all of your particular habits of thought, each individual's journey to this kind of consciousness is unique. To do this consciously and deliberately involves some form of mindfulness meditation, in which you become centered in your own awareness (see, for instance, the second practice at the end of chapter two on creative mind). This is not so much a practice of stopping your thoughts; rather, it is about remaining present and aware, regardless of whether there are passing thoughts or not. True creative freedom takes place in "the space between thoughts."

The New Age catch phrase that "you create your reality"— i.e., you create your own *experience* of reality—is indeed true, at least within the context of these seven principles. But the exciting and inspiring *promise* implicit in this idea, the promise that you can fulfill and manifest the truth of your desires—the experience of ever-expanding well-being—cannot be realized unless you shift to a different level of consciousness. You are indeed co-creating your experience *all* of the time. But as long as you identify with a limited and conditioned "you," you are, at least in large part, creating on automatic pilot and subconsciously following the same basic routines and habits that you have always followed.

You can *freely* co-create your reality only when *you* have become free and unconditioned, only when you have shifted your focus to the level of pure awareness. In a sense, you can fulfill and manifest the truth of your desires only when you are no longer "you," only when you have ceased to identify with that made-up character in your mind, and have shifted your attention to mind itself. The time and effort involved in this shift of focus will be directly proportional to how much you currently identify with that conditioned "you" and how lost you are in the drama of your life.

Your identification with the conditioned "you" is reflected in such things as your attachment to your body and its pleasures and pains; to particular worldly circumstances, such as fame or money or power; to your opinions of right and wrong; to your personal history (your story of all of your accomplishments, and all of your scars and wounds); to your judgments and grievances; to your own unwillingness to forgive; to your fears and anger and unhappiness; and most subtle of all, to your allegiance to all of your rationalizations for these attachments. It is also reflected as your habits of thought and feeling, which tend to lock you into a given quality of life experience.

Every time you indulge in these attachments, you are strengthening that identification in your mind—you are identifying yourself with one of the thoughts in your awareness, rather than with the awareness itself. By doing this, you limit your possibilities of experience to what is consistent with this thought construct of "you." In effect you are seeing the world only as it is reflected in the mirror of your past—that is to say, in the mirror of *the story you are telling yourself* about your past. In doing this, you are not doing anything "wrong" or "bad." But you are limiting your own experience and your own happiness.

Regardless of the particular form of your desire, what you really desire is the joy and fulfillment of creatively expressing your truth, creatively extending and manifesting love and well-being. Each particular thing or circumstance you desire is simply a symbol for this exuberant self-expression. The particular symbols that you desire will depend on your self-concept.

A limited or false self-concept will give rise to limited desires—desires whose manifestation will be accompanied only by limited happiness at best. For instance, if you completely identity with the limited conditioned "you" that believes it is incomplete and must somehow get what it needs from the external world, then your desires will be limited to those worldly things and conditions you think will "make" you feel happy and safe and complete. The scope of your conscious desires will be limited by your own limited self-concept. How would *your* desires change if you knew you had no lack, no needs, no fears and no limitations?

From the perspective of your deeper truth as a be-ing of creative mind, you know that you are already complete. You are free of any imagined needs, and free to joyfully express your own overflowing creative abundance. As you become more aware of your own truth as a be-ing of creative mind—i.e., more Self-aware—you will also become more aware of your true desires. For instance, as you become more Self-aware, your desires extend to more fully include the happiness and well-being of others, since you are no longer feeling insecure or afraid for your own well-being.

What makes a desire a "true desire" is the state of mind of the desirer and not what is being desired. The crucial issue is whether the desires arise from a deeper Self-awareness or from a limited, needy self-concept. The particular form of the desire doesn't really matter.

It makes no difference whether the object of your desire is material or non-material. For instance, you might desire a relationship from that "place" in your mind of perfect peace and happiness. You would joyfully desire the relationship as a way to more joyfully express your truth as the giving and receiving of love. Or, you might desire a relationship from a place of imagined need—a desperate grasping for another person to fulfill some imagined lack in yourself. This is the "I can't live without you" version of romantic love.

Likewise, it is entirely possible that the desire for something like a new car could be a true desire. Again, if the desire arises from Self-awareness and happiness, then the manifestation of that desire will reflect and symbolize that happiness. But if the desire arises from a limited self-concept of need and lack, its manifestation will not, in and of itself, make you happy. In fact, its manifestation might even aggravate your sense of unhappiness. This is illustrated in all of the fairy tales of magic lamps and genies, in which the hero wishes for all the wrong things. To quote the words of a popular song, it is like "looking for love in all the wrong places."

From the perspective of creative mind, the manifestation of something—i.e., your *experience* of that thing, which includes what it means to you—is not caused by some external reality. Ultimately, that experience is a creative expression of your thoughts. The happiness or unhappiness associated with any manifestation is simply a reflection of the state of mind of the person doing the manifesting. In and of itself, *a manifestation has no independent power to make you happy or unhappy.* Happiness always comes from within. *You bring happiness to your manifestations—you don't get happiness from them.*

Allowing Manifestation

Your desires arise spontaneously. The infinite creative potential for love spontaneously translates those desires into experiences. From the perspective of these seven principles, this is simply the eternal creative truth. But your own mind's openness and ability to *experience* this eternal creative process depends on your thoughts and beliefs. Source-like or allowing beliefs allow your mind to experience the manifestations of its true desires.

Un-source-like or restricting beliefs restrict your mind's ability to experience those manifestations. Strictly speaking, the phrase "experience the manifestations" is redundant, since "to manifest my desires" *means* that I experience being or having what I want. But the phrase emphasizes that what my thoughts are actually allowing or restricting is my own mind's openness, rather than exerting power over source's creativity.

So it turns out that manifesting, like being happy, is a matter of allowing—joyful active allowing—rather than somehow "making" your dreams come true. And in the final analysis, how to allow manifestation is the same as how to allow happiness. In the simplest terms, you allow manifestation when you think happy thoughts. You disallow manifestation when you think unhappy thoughts. And what you are allowing or disallowing is your own mind's ability to experience manifestation.

There are typically two kinds of negative and restricting thoughts that limit your ability to experience the manifestation of your true desires. The first are thoughts of a limited or threatening external reality. For instance, you believe that you cannot have what you desire because there is not enough to go around, or that others are somehow keeping your good from you, or that the political or economic circumstances of your life simply will not allow you to realize your dreams. As we have seen, these kinds of thoughts are all based on the belief in separation, in which you mistake yourself and others as passive and vulnerable beings instead of creative minds.

The second kind of limiting or restricting thoughts are your thoughts of self-judgment and self-condemnation. This includes thoughts that you are not good enough or talented enough or lucky enough to have what you desire. That may be simply an expression of your fear and insecurity that somehow you are not adequate or worthy. You may even think that this lack of self-love is actually a virtue, believing that self-denigration is a form of noble humility.

These thoughts of self-judgment and self-condemnation are ultimately forms of not loving yourself, of withholding love from yourself. Withholding love from yourself is actually a denial of your own truth as a be-ing of universal and unconditional love. You *are* an extension of source, an expression of the infinite creative potential for well-being. Your happiness, which necessarily includes your unconditional self-acceptance and self-love, *is* the on-going creative fulfillment of source's nature. Your happiness *is* source's happiness, *is* the fulfillment and expression of source's eternal extending-forth of love.

One way you express your nature of universal love is by *allowing* yourself to be happy and to experience the fulfillment of your desires. The first step in this allowing is an undoing. You undo or let go of restricting thoughts of limitation and inadequacy and unworthiness. You stop doing whatever restricts your awareness of the truth of love and prevents you from self-awarely being yourself.

Affirmations and visualizations can sometimes be effective tools to undo or reverse limiting thoughts. But this must be distinguished from a popular approach that I call "desperate efforting." This approach prescribes a strict regimen of visualization and affirmation that you must follow to "make" your dreams come true. And it warns you that if you don't follow the program religiously, your dreams won't come true at all. It is similar to getting one of those e-mails that says if you pass it on to all of your friends, then something good will happen to you.

But if you fail to pass it on, then something awful will happen (or at the very least, you will have forever missed your chance at the something good).

Visualization and affirmation can indeed be wonderful and valuable tools, if they are practiced without fear. But we want to remember when creative mind co-creates with loving source, we don't have to somehow "make" our desires manifest at all. We have only to stop preventing them from manifesting. We have only to *allow* our minds to manifest, only to *allow* ourselves to experience loving source naturally fulfilling our loving desires. The only thing we have to actually "do" is to simply be ourselves—to be happy and extend love.

Everyone Wins

One way a limited self-concept reveals itself is when we find ourselves thinking in terms of one person's gain at the expense of another's loss. By thinking that the only possibilities in a situation are that either I gain (and you lose) OR you gain (and I lose), I am implicitly denying and hiding the possibilities in which we both win, we both experience happiness and well-being. (What we are discussing here is different from the winning and losing involved in a game or a sports competition. In the present context, we are talking about "winning" and "losing" in terms of happiness. Simply scoring fewer points in a game obviously does not mean that you have to be unhappy.)

When I see only the possibilities of either gaining OR losing, my happiness will be limited at best. If I think that I have "won," the happiness of my "getting" may be tainted by a vague sense of guilt or unease over "taking" from another. In truth, I haven't really taken anything from another, nor could I. But as long as

I believe that I have, I will feel, at least implicitly, some degree of unhappiness. Of course, if I think that I have "lost," then I will obviously feel unhappy.

Moreover, to whatever extent I reinforce the whole idea of conflict and competition in the mind of the other, I will also reinforce her own sense of unhappiness as well, regardless of whether she thinks she has won or lost.

From the perspective of one power, seeing a situation in terms of conflict and competition is always a wake-up call. It is an opportunity to step back from the drama for a moment, and to refocus your attention on the truth of one power.

In most religious traditions, there is some version of the prayer, "Let God's Will be done." In our one-power way of thinking, we might say "Let source-power become manifest in our awareness." The one power or cause in all of reality is love—love ever-extending itself. This creative impulse or thrust toward ever-expanding well-being could be called the "will" of love. Love's will is ultimately the *only* will, the only creative force. From this perspective, "Let source-power become manifest in our awareness" could be translated as "Let love's will become manifest in our awareness." In any particular situation of seeming conflict and competition, I would be asking that deeper part of my awareness to show me a way in which everyone could win, everyone could experience happiness and well-being. Being open to that possibility is a shift of my attention from an egocentric to a source-centric awareness. That shift is essential both to realizing my full potential for happiness and well-being, and to helping others realize theirs.

From the perspective of one power, the possibility of everyone winning—everyone finding well-being, happiness, abundance, and love—*is* the ultimate truth of every situation. There is only one power, one truth for all beings. The full creative manifestation of that power is the ever-expanding well-being of everyone.

Indeed, when I have used this prayer—when I have truly allowed myself to sink deeply into the state of mind of "Let love's will become manifest in our awareness"—I have found that it invariably had a healing effect on situations of conflict and struggle. It not only changed my perception from conflict to harmony and from fear to love, but it also somehow caused a shift in the other person's perceptions as well. New possibilities of win-win became apparent to both of us, and feelings of animosity were spontaneously replaced by feelings of friendship and good will. This is not something that "I" do "to" others, as if I were exerting my power "over" the conflict, or "over" the other person's mind. Thinking of it like that would simply be an expression of a belief in two powers. Rather, this shift of perception happens when I give my mind over completely to the idea of the *one* power of perfect love. And this healing shift of my own mind seems to open up the possibility for the healing shift in the other person's mind.

A Healing Shift of Perception

I have found that the prayer or meditation of "Let love's will become manifest in our awareness" also causes a healing shift of the perception of physical illness. For example, if I am feeling sick, and I am able to sink deeply into this one-power kind of consciousness, I almost always feel better. I can't say that it works completely every time I do it. But I believe that this is a reflection of my own inability to completely make that shift of mind, rather than any inconsistency in the principle itself.

Moreover, when another person is feeling sick and I use this prayer to shift my mind into a one-power kind of consciousness, often their pain or sickness gets better or even goes away—sometimes even dramatically and instantly. Again, this is not something that "I" am doing "to" them, as if I am exerting my power "over" some sickness power, or even "over" the other person's mental state. To think of it in that way would simply be another version of the belief in two powers. Rather, the healing shift happens when I give my mind over completely to the idea of the *one* power of perfect love. And when one individualized expression of creative mind remembers the truth of one love, it opens that possibility for other expressions of mind. In the language of some mystical traditions, when one self remembers the truth of Self, it opens that possibility for other selves.

To avoid any misunderstanding here, I am definitely not saying that we should never seek medical (or chiropractic, natu-ropathic, etc.) help when we are sick. Ultimately I do believe that if I completely knew my inner truth and were completely confident in this knowing, there would be nothing that would not heal with this shift of consciousness. Moreover, from within this level of awareness, there would be no experience of any real problem that needed healing. But in the level of consciousness in which I and most everyone else are living now, this is not yet the case. So I sometimes do seek professional health care if I believe I need to.

If the question arises within you, "Maybe I should see a doctor this time—maybe this is a 'real' illness, and not just an illusory projected experience," then there is still some level of dualism in your core beliefs. You still harbor some degree of the belief that your body is an external reality that can threaten or even destroy your mind's experience of well-being. That belief will be creatively reflected as the experience of an external thing that has some power over you. You will think that you need some material kind of intervention to fix your body, to make it well so that it doesn't make you suffer or even die. And thoughts like these will have corresponding experiential reflections. Another way to say this is that if not seeking medical help would increase your fear, then you probably should go to the doctor. Any increase of fear will tend to be reflected as more sickness and suffering.

When you project thoughts of separation and victimhood, your experiences will serve to validate those thoughts for you. Projective mind always provides its own proof. For instance, if you believe that your sense of well-being is at the mercy of your body—which you think of as some real thing that exists external to your mind—then your mind will make experiences of sickness and suffering to validate that belief. Your experience of your body acting *against* your desires "proves" that your belief in externality and victimhood was right.

But from the perspective of creative mind, your projected beliefs are being creatively translated into experiences that reflect those beliefs. Relatively speaking, the thoughts are the cause and the experiences are the effects. So your experiences cannot "prove" the validity of your beliefs—rather, your experiences are simply the creative reflections of your beliefs. And if you don't like your experiences, you need to change the mind of the experiencer.

Likewise, when I am helping others, I always advise them to seek whatever professional care that they feel they need. For the past twenty years, I have been a network chiropractor. I help patients through chiropractic spinal adjustments, and I offer nutritional and exercise advice. But I offer this physical help from within a frame of mind that recognizes the essential innate wholeness of each person. I even tell my patients at the outset of care that there is a perfect healing power within them, and that it is our job to remove the blockages to the expression of that power. I believe that this vision of their perfect inner health is an essential part of their healing. But a certain degree of physical interaction is still necessary, given their level of consciousness as well as my own. That physical interaction allows healing to take place without threatening their beliefs about the fundamental nature of physical reality. They can tell themselves that they are getting well because the right things were done to their bodies to remove the physical blockages to health.

At the deepest level, I believe that healing could be instantaneous and without any physical intervention at all. But most of the time such a healing would be so much at odds with our core beliefs about our bodies and the nature of reality, that we would be terrified. And the one power of love, which is the source of every experience of healing, never acts to increase fear. Fear would only manifest as further experiences of sickness and lack.

From the perspective of these seven principles, your greatest contribution to the healing of yourself and others is to shift into or surrender to that deeper level of consciousness where you *know* that there are no real problems that need to be healed—that every problem is simply a mistaken and illusory perception. Your role is not to struggle against perceived problems, or to exert your mental power over them, or even to understand and explain where these illusions came from. Your role is to simply hold the vision of the truth, the truth of the one power of love. In that state of mind, you are not looking at or thinking about the problems at all, nor about "healing" those problems. You are not thinking about what should happen in the process of healing or what the end result should look like. Ultimately, the healing is as much of an illusion as the problem—the "healing" is simply the illusory undoing of the illusion of "a problem that needs to be healed." Your role is to focus wholly and completely on the truth of the one power of love. That focus will allow your mind and other minds to shift their perceptions from un-source-like perceptions of conflict, suffering, fear and unhappiness to source-like perceptions of peace, well-being, love and joy.

In some cases, simply being in this meditative healing state of mind is enough to cause a shift of the other person's perception. In other cases, we may need something more to allow our minds to make a healing shift. That something more could be as simple as a heartfelt smile or a kind word. Or it could be as complex as brain surgery. But the first step of all true healing is to move into that deeper prayerful state of peace and trust.

Remember that this practice is not about reciting a magic formula to somehow change the world or solve a problem. From the perspective of one power, there is no external objective world that we have to change. There are only our experiences, both individual and collective. To change our experience of the world, we need to change the level of consciousness of the experiencer—change it from a separative level to a one-power level.

For me, this meditative prayer of "Let love's will become manifest in our awareness" helps me to make that shift. "Let" means that it's something that I'm allowing rather than doing. "Love's will" implies that there is only one power and that power is love. "Become manifest" suggests that love and happiness and well-being are eternally the truth, and it is only a matter of allowing ourselves to become aware of it. Nothing real needs to change—we just have to see more clearly. And finally, "in our awareness" reminds me that this becoming manifest will express itself as the peace and joy and well-being of everyone involved. Even my initial thought of "There's something wrong in my life or another's, and I need to say this prayer" is an expression of some degree of unpeace in my own mind, a reflection of the belief that there is a real problem that needs to be solved.

In my experience, this way of shifting my mind works—it causes a healing shift of my perceptions and the perceptions of others. But ironically, it is when the appearances no longer matter at all that they seem to change. The shift of perception comes about when I no longer care about any shift of perception, when I am no longer concerned with changing the perceptions of myself and others.

In the end, this kind of shift is the joyful manifestation that we all truly desire. The key to this joyful manifestation is shifting the consciousness of the manifestor into a level of perfect peace and perfect joy.

"Miracles"

From the perspective of one power, a "miracle" is simply a shift in perception. Since love is the only power, every perception of a "problem"—every perception of evil or suffering in yourself or another—is a misperception, a distortion caused by your restricting thoughts. Love eternally offers *only* the possibility of perfect well-being, and this is the *only* possibility that is offered. But your restricting thoughts make your mind incapable of receiving or experiencing perfect well-being. A "miracle" is a shift in perception—a shift from closed-off-ness to openness, from distortion to clarity, from the illusion of separation, sin and suffering to seeing the truth of love.

This does not mean that there is some real external material world of perfect goodness that we can see only after we have stopped restricting our awareness. To better understand this, we can distinguish between the form and the content of our perception.

From the perspective of one power, love is the only creative power, and love creates by extending itself. Therefore the only true content of perception must be love. The form of perception—i.e., what particular things you see, who says or does what to whom, etc.—depends on how your thoughts and beliefs interact with the truth of love. When you are seeing clearly and without the distortion of restricting thoughts, you will perceive only love, only well-being, only peace, only perfection—regardless of the form of your perception. You may experience the presence of love in the form of a sunset, a child, a tree, a piece of music, a smile. You may even experience the presence of love and perfection in the "distorted" form of a person apparently dying of cancer, or one person apparently attacking or harming another. The forms of perception are always changing, but the truth of love never changes. You know you are seeing the truth of love when you feel perfect peace and happiness. And in those moments of clarity, "what" you are perceiving is love. The particular forms you are perceiving are irrelevant.

We can contrast that kind of perception—seeing the unchanging content of love within all of the changing forms— with what we have called the "distorted" perception of a two-power way of thinking. A two-power way of thinking perceives only the forms of perception, only the projections of its own restrictive thoughts. For that perspective, there is no other dimension of perception. In effect, the form of perception *is* the content. For instance, when that way of thinking perceives an apparently sick person, it sees only the real objective presence of sickness. It does not consider that the apparent sickness is only a shadow cast by its own *idea* of sickness—its own *idea* of a second power, a power for un-well-being, a power that opposes love.

The shift of perception involved in a miracle is a shift from being lost in the dualistic projected forms of perception to seeing the unchanging content of love. That is the essence of the miracle. The real change is in the perceiver—essentially a change from fear to love, from unpeace to peace, from unhappiness to perfect happiness. The forms of perception may or may not change. But it turns out that often the forms of perception do change—sickness miraculously changes into wellness, lack miraculous changes into abundance.

Moreover, the shift of perception involved in a miracle can extend beyond the perceiver to another person. When you are seeing only the content of love in another, the other's perception can also change. He may experience a miraculous shift from unpeace to peace, from fear to love. And it can even affect the forms of his perception. For instance, he may miraculously experience a healing of his sickness. Somehow when you truly allow love's will to manifest in your awareness, you enable the other to allow it to manifest in his awareness. I confess that I don't understand exactly "how" this happens. But I have absolutely no doubt that it does happen.

The word "miracle" implies two things. First, that you experience a *healing* change, a change for the better. Second, this change seems to be outside of the normal causal laws of the world. For instance, a sick person might spontaneously and instantly become well, rather than slowly becoming well over a period of time while taking medications. There is no "natural" explanation for the occurrence, if "natural" means "following the known scientific laws of cause and effect in the material world."

It should be noted that for the one-power perspective, however, miracles are completely "natural." A miracle is simply the shift of perception that occurs when you stop restricting your own awareness. From this perspective, it is the perception of sin and suffering and fear that is "unnatural," because that indicates you are blocking your awareness of the presence of love. And *only* love is truly present at all.

There is never any way to "prove" that a miracle has occurred, that a perceived change in the world was not either a random coincidence or merely an effect of a scientific law of causality. Did the cancer miraculously disappear, or was the initial diagnosis simply wrong? Or was it the effect of the chemotherapy interacting with the patient's particular genetic make-up in a way that we don't yet understand? There is no way to prove that a miracle occurred. But there is also no way to prove that a miracle did not occur.

In my own experience, however, there is always an element of inner certainty involved in a "miracle experience"—an inner *knowing* that something miraculous has occurred. Again, there's no way to "prove" that a miracle occurred, no way to "prove" that I'm not just fooling myself. But there is a sense of inner knowing that is very different from mere thinking or speculation—you simply know that you know.

An Example of a Healing Miracle

At the urging of both my wife and my editor, I'm going to share an example of a miracle from my own experience. I was very resistant to doing this because it was so intensely personal and profound for me. I didn't want to turn it into just another anecdote. But these people (especially my wife) were relentless, and I finally gave in. They convinced me that sharing this story might be helpful for others. But it is important for me to at least mention my reservations.

First, I don't want to present this as an illustration of how "special" I am. It is very common for authors and speakers to emphasize their specialness as a way to establish credibility. For instance, they speak about special powers they have, or special communications with "the other side," or special experiences they have had in their childhood. In a world that is hungry for teachers and gurus, these claims of specialness are welcomed as a sure sign that the person is indeed an authority. I am not criticizing the truly wonderful gifts that many of these teachers have. But I don't want this book to be accepted because the reader thinks that I am somehow special. I think your true guru is within you, and that what I share can be at best a way to remember and reconnect with your own inner knowing.

I agree with *A Course in Miracles* that the idea of specialness is the primary obstacle to our awareness of the presence of love, and is responsible for our unhappiness. The essence and foundation of a miracle experience is that we are somehow interconnected, somehow one, somehow the same. And when one of us surrenders to this shared truth, it affects everyone else who is lost in the illusion of being separate and special. The "healing" that takes place is ultimately a shift in awareness, and not a change in an external world—it is a releasing of the distortions caused by restrictive separative thought. And anything that reinforces the ideas of separateness and difference and specialness actually prevents that healing shift.

It's never a matter of "taking credit" for a miracle. For instance in the example below, it was not a miracle that "Bill" did. It was the shift of awareness that occurred for both Bill and other people when Bill temporarily gave up being Bill. My role in the whole experience was my complete surrender of any thought of specialness, any thought of having a separate will. This has nothing to do with me having a special ability. It is something that anyone can do, although in my experience it does take a certain amount of commitment and discipline to let go of the ego even temporarily (which is the best I've been able to do so far). I believe that this non-specialness is important for any idea or teaching that aspires to be universal. In other words, you don't have to see auras or channel other-worldly entities or have childhood mystical experiences to understand or use what I am saying. If you do have any of these wonderful abilities, use them well, and don't let them deteriorate into mere distractions or advertisements for your own ego. But if you don't seem to have any extraordinary abilities, don't worry about it. You can still have all that you truly desire—you can awaken, you can experience perfect peace and happiness, you can experience miracles and offer miracles to others.

Second, what I really want is for you, the reader, to try this for yourself and discover whatever truth you can in whatever way is most appropriate for you. By giving examples, I run the risk of somehow prejudicing the reader, especially if he doesn't believe or like my particular example. And then he may not try it for himself. And so I was reluctant to give any actual examples that a skeptical reader might use as an excuse to "debunk" the whole idea.

Or if you like my example, you might try to get the same result that I did. But this process is not about trying to get a particular outcome. It is about surrendering to love's will. You don't and can't know what outcome is the best for everyone involved. Sometimes the greatest healing may be a peaceful death. This process is about lovingly surrendering yourself to love's will, without any attachment to the outcome.

So those are my reservations and qualifications and cautions, the "grain of salt" with which you should read this story.

In this example, I used the prayer "Let love's will become manifest in our awareness"—or perhaps it would be more appropriate to say that I allowed that prayer to use me. In my experience, this prayer can be a vehicle for miraculous healing effects, a vehicle that can allow a miraculous shift in perception in both my awareness and in others' awareness.

Experiences like this cannot be accurately described in words. At best, words can point toward the place within your own mind where such an experience is possible. Everyone's experience with this prayer will be different, since everyone's mind and inner journey to the truth are unique.

Using this prayer as my guide, I allow my mind to settle more and more deeply into the silence. Typically I am thinking about the prayer in the beginning. Then gradually I find myself thinking less and less. And then there is a gap of some kind, a discontinuity in my self-awareness that I realize only after I am aware again. And when I become self-aware again, there is a sense of deep peace in which I *know*—not believe, but know—that love is the only truth regardless of appearances. I *know* that all is well, whether or not the sickness goes away, whether or not the person lives or dies. Even to say "I" know is misleading—my mind is simply aware of the knowing. And once my mind is aware of the truth of the perfect goodness of what is, I no longer feel any need to pray—for what could one possibly pray for when he *knows* that there is only love? That shift of perspective is the miracle. And any changes in the forms of my perceptions and the forms of others' perceptions—those changes are simply the effects of the miracle.

Early one evening, I learned that the child of one of my patients had been involved in a horrendous accident. (Note that even calling this "horrendous" was a reflection of my own limited and fearful thinking at the time.) Given the particulars of the accident, it was unbelievable that the child had survived at all. She had to be airlifted to another city to undergo extensive surgery and reconstruction, with little or no hope of success. I took this news very hard. I had known the parents and the grandparents of the child for years. I was overwhelmed with sadness for the child and the parents and the grandparents. I felt such an ache in my heart that it was hard to breathe. Even reliving these feelings now brings tears to my eyes.

I was distracted all evening, but I didn't know anything that I could do. And feeling so helpless only made the sense of anguish worse. Finally I went to bed for the night. But about three or four in the morning I awoke from a restless sleep. I simply couldn't stay in bed. And so I got up and I did what I always do when I'm at the end of my rope: I prayed.

I used the prayer, "Let love's will become manifest in our awareness." I sunk into the idea of the one power of love. I asked that this trust in love would be manifest in my awareness as peace. As long as I was lost in the "awful tragedy" of others' pain and suffering, I felt no peace. And I asked that love's will become manifest in the awareness of the parents and the grandparents, that they feel peace, that they *know* that all is eternally well regardless of appearances. And I asked that the child experience peace, even in the midst of her pain.

At first, this prayer seemed futile to me. The injuries were so severe and extensive. The pain of the parents and grandparents was so deep and overwhelming. My own sadness was so overpowering. How was it possible for anyone to feel peace or joy in such a horrible situation? But I continued to lose myself in the prayer, continued to affirm and re-affirm the truth of love in the hope that I would come to feel it, to know it.

I still have no idea how long this process went on. I lost myself in wanting peace and healing for my friends and the child. At some point, there was no longer a "me" wanting this to happen—there was only the deep longing of my heart. And gradually there was less and less thought, less and less conscious wanting. There was only silence. I have no idea how long the silence lasted, since there was no conscious "I" keeping track.

Then I was aware that there was *only* love—that there eternally *is only* love. I *knew* this with absolute certainty. I *knew* that there was no reason to be sad or upset, regardless of appearances. I *knew* that *all* was well. I *knew* that the child and the parents and the grandparents were perfectly OK, regardless of all appearances of injury or even death. I felt only peace, only love, only a deep sense of joy. I knew then that I had "done my part" in this unfolding drama, and I went back to bed peacefully in the certainty that all was well. All was eternally well, and that wellness could never possibly change, no matter what experiences we might have to the contrary.

The next day I talked with the grandmother by phone. She told me that the child had died and been revived twice during the night. But then in the early morning hours she had "miraculously" turned the corner and was out of danger. None of the doctors or nurses could explain it. By all indications, there was simply no way that the child could possibly have survived at all. But she did. And everyone in the hospital called it a "miracle."

When I heard that, I cried—cried tears of gratitude and joy. Even now remembering this story is very emotional for me. When I heard this news, I *knew* that my prayer—or rather, my surrendering to prayer—had played a role in her miraculous recovery. Nothing that I could ever prove, but I *knew*. But I also knew that her recovery and survival were at some level irrelevant. I knew that all was well, that there was only the power of love, regardless of whether she had lived or died.

I also knew that somehow my own allowing—allowing love's will to manifest in my awareness, and extending that allowing to the other people involved—had enabled their allowing. It had somehow enabled them to become aware of love's presence.

And as a wonderful footnote, in the subsequent weeks and months the young girl not only survived but recovered almost fully, with virtually no lingering effects from the "horrendous" accident.

"Little" Everyday Miracles

Why is "little" in quotes? Because when you read this next example, it may seem so trivial that you might think it shouldn't be included in a section about miracles at all. But ultimately I don't believe there are bigger and smaller miracles. A miracle is a shift of perception that allows us to experience the presence of love. Period. The apparent size or degree of a miracle is only relative to the distortion that we were making before the shift— only relative to the apparent size or degree of the "problem." But from the perspective of one power, that problem is unreal, is only a misperception. And our belief that some problems are bigger than others is ultimately just part of the illusion.

I'm including the example of this "everyday miracle" to emphasize that a miraculous shift of perception is always possible. It does not depend on first perceiving some "horrible" tragedy or unfairness. Any time you are not experiencing *perfect* peace and happiness, a miracle is possible. *A miracle is always just one thought away.* And I think appreciating the "little" miracles available in every moment allows us to more fully offer and experience the "big" miracles. In other words, as we become more and more certain that there *is* only love, we are less and less intimidated by the many illusory forms of fear regardless of their illusory sizes and degrees.

The other reason I am sharing this story is that it is an example of a miracle that I played no conscious role in at all. I was not praying or meditating or intending to shift my own or another's perception. The miraculous shift of my perception simply happened. Perhaps I was just in an especially receptive state of mind that day. It was actually a very common everyday experience that almost everyone has now and then. But this experience helped me to understand miracles at a deeper level. This time I recognized that it was a miracle instead of just taking it for granted.

My wife and I were visiting our daughter and son-in-law and new grandson for the weekend. On Sunday morning I awoke early, and headed out to get a cup of coffee and go the local Target store to pick up a few things. There was nothing special about the morning—just a typical grey overcast fall morning on Long Island. I arrived at the store early and there were only a few customers and a few store clerks in the huge building. But it was one of those mornings where everything seemed just perfect. The colors were especially bright and beautiful. The items on the shelves seemed just right. Each person I saw in the store seemed perfect just the way they were. I walked through the empty aisles smiling at the magnificence of it all.

And then it hit me. There was nothing special about this experience, at least in any "objective" sense. It was just a Target store, pretty much a carbon copy of similar stores all over the country. But what was different was my state of mind. Somehow I was receptive to see the beauty and the perfection of everything. This was not a mystical experience of a great white light and the oneness of all Being. Just a perception of an "ordinary" situation seen as perfect just the way it was. In that moment, I felt only perfect peace and happiness.

Everyone I've shared this story with has had similar experiences, so I know that it is not a rare occurrence. But there's something important in this. I believe that the "everything-is-perfect" quality is *always* present—more precisely, the *possibility* of perceiving everything as perfect is always present, always offered by source. But we notice it only when we are receptive—either because our usual resistance is somehow momentarily suspended, or because we are actively cultivating our receptivity in that moment. A miracle is the shift of perception that allows us to realize the ever-offered and ever-present possibility of being aware of the presence of love.

Ultimately, miracles will cease to occur when we are completely receptive and we are aware of *only* the presence of love in everything we perceive. A miracle, after all, is a shift in our perception from illusion to awareness. A miracle exists only within the context of our restrictive thoughts, only within the context of our lack of receptivity, only within the context of the illusion of the absence of love. But until we experience *only* love, our role is to actively cultivate our receptivity and extend that receptivity to others—to actively offer miracles to ourselves and others.

From a certain perspective, this story of going to the Target store may seem trivial in comparison with the "miraculous recovery from death" example. But I believe they illustrate the same thing. The possibility of experiencing perfect well-being, perfect joy and perfect peace is possible in every moment, if we can but allow ourselves to be aware of it. And the more we allow it—the more we actively cultivate our receptivity—the more we will experience miracles in our lives. And the more we will be able to extend miracles to others.

From the perspective of one power, the possibility of experiencing miracles is offered to us in *every* moment. In fact, it is the *only* possibility offered ever. And it is our life purpose to allow ourselves and others to realize that possibility.

For me, the prayer of "Let love's will become manifest in our awareness" is one of the most effective ways I know to make this miraculous shift of consciousness for myself and to help others to make it for themselves. In the chapters that follow, we will see how forgiveness and appreciation and love are also powerful tools to open our minds to the presence of love. Will this work for you in your own life? Find out.

Practicing the Principle of Joyful Manifestation

1 Stop for a moment and sit quietly. Let go of all of your beliefs in lack and need. Realize that you are a be-ing of the infinite eternal creative potential for well-being. There is nothing that you could get or do that could add to or subtract from the everything you already are. Realize that your desires are not for satisfying needs but are rather expressing your overflowing creative abundance. How does this perspective change what you desire? How does it change how the whole process of desiring feels?

2 As often as you can remember to do it today, ask yourself, "What form do I want to give to the power of ever-expanding goodness now?" When you experience something seemingly negative in your life, look at it as an opportunity to re-focus your attention on what you desire now, rather than feeling unhappy or anxious about what you don't want.

3 Whenever you are in a situation with another person in which you can see only two mutually exclusive possibilities—either you winning (and the other losing), OR the other winning (and you losing)—ask a deeper part of your mind to reveal a third possibility in which you both can win. You may find it helpful to use the prayer or meditation, "Let love's will become manifest in our awareness." Let your mind sink deeply into the idea of one power, the thought that there is only one cause and one will, and that is for the perfect well-being of every mind. How does this change how you see

the situation? How you feel about the situation? What new possibilities do you discover? How does it change the state of mind and the behavior of the other person?

Also, whenever you are in a situation where you or another is experiencing sickness or suffering or fear, use this prayer, "Let love's will become manifest in our awareness." Let your mind sink deeply into the idea of the one power of perfect love. How does this shift your own perceptions? How does it shift the perceptions of the other person?

Remember that this practice is not about reciting a magic formula to somehow change the world or solve a problem. Your goal is not to heal the world but rather to heal your own mind. Even if you start the practice with some thought about the problem or person you hope to help, you want to let yourself become so wholly and completely focused on love's will itself that there is no awareness of anything else at all. There is only peace.

Again, don't think of this practice as a substitute for seeking whatever medical help you feel is necessary. Think of it rather as the first essential step on your or another's healing journey. And then take whatever other steps you feel are called for.

FORGIVENESS IS FREEDOM

When we forgive, we free ourselves and others from the illusion of guilt and fear. We free ourselves and others to co-create a life experience of perfect happiness, perfect peace and unconditional love.

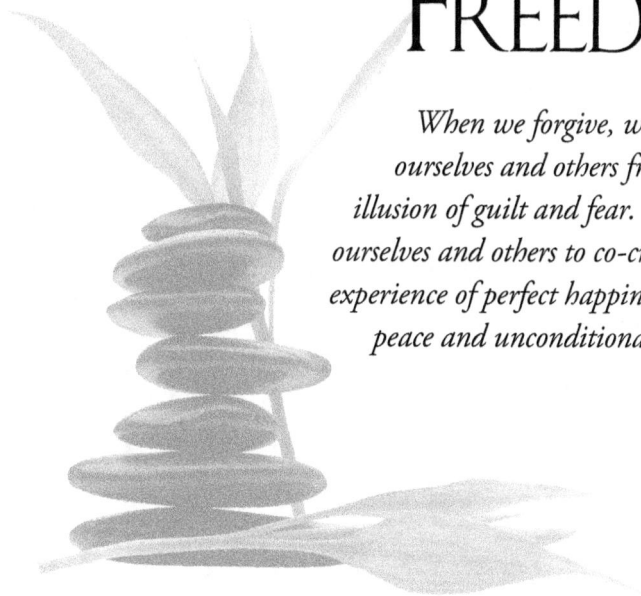

Forgiveness is a topic that is central to most religious and spiritual beliefs. But often forgiveness can seem to us—especially when we are in the very midst of (seemingly very justified) anger and judgment—to be giving up something important. It often seems as if being angry and judging is simply "normal," and is our "right" (especially when we are "in the right"). It seems that holding a grievance can be a good thing, because it reminds us to keep our guard up against those who could take away our happiness and well-being. Many people would even claim that judging and condemning what is bad in the world is a moral responsibility. Far from helping us to be happier, it can often seem that forgiveness is actually a kind of sacrifice on our parts—a sacrifice that we might we willing to make because we "should," or a sacrifice that will earn us a reward later, but a sacrifice nonetheless.

But when you understand forgiveness within the context of these seven principles, it will come to mean something very different. Forgiveness turns out to be absolutely essential to allowing happiness. Forgiveness *is* freedom—ultimately your own freedom to clearly and deeply manifest the truth of love in the form of happy feelings and experiences.

Projection and Extension

Your experience is a reflection of your thoughts. *A Course in Miracles* notes that thoughts can be creatively translated into experience in one of two ways, by "projection" or by "extension." This is a very helpful distinction, although my definition and use of these terms below reflect my own interpretation.

The most common process is projection. This is where we all start, and often stay our entire lives. Projection is a subconscious process of interpretation. You are unaware that you have actively interpreted the world, and you believe that the reality and the meaning that you experience are simply "out there." *Projection is interpretation parading as objective reality.* In fact, the very notion of "objectivity" is projective, since it assumes that there is some way of looking at and experiencing the world that is free of interpretation. Projection always involves some belief in separation and externality, some idea that there is a separate external world out there with its own meaning and value in itself.

One of the best examples of projection is blame. When I am unhappy, I tend to projectively interpret things and people and events in the world as being the causes of my unhappiness. But because I am unaware of doing this, I believe that someone or something else really did cause my unhappiness. I project blame onto the world, and then I experience the world and others as bad or guilty.

In contrast to projection, extension is a *conscious* process of interpretation. For instance, many of the suggested practices in this book are exercises in extending a new interpretation onto some part of your life experience. In extending a thought, you are self-aware of your necessary and inevitable role in co-creating your experience. You realize your identity as creative mind, and you fully own your responsibility for the meaning and form of your experience. You realize that your experience is a reflection of your thoughts. When you are not satisfied with what you are experiencing, you need to change the cause rather than trying to manipulate or control the effects. You deliberately and self-awarely change your thoughts, your focus of attention and your state of mind, rather than battling with or complaining about their experiential reflections. Whenever you experience darkness in the world, your response is to extend more light.

Judgment and Projection

A "judgment" is a belief that something external to you, in and of itself, has the power to affect your well-being positively or negatively, to cause you to experience good or harm, and to make you happy or unhappy. *Every judgment is a projection*— an unconscious interpretation in which you see the world as an independent power, and yourself as a victim (or perhaps a beneficiary).

All judgments involve an element of fear, because they reflect the belief that your well-being is somehow dependent on the whim of some being or force outside your awareness. They reflect the belief that the quality of your life experience is outside your control.

Negative judgments, such as grudges and grievances, obviously involve fear. If I believe that I am being attacked or threatened by others outside my mind, then I feel afraid or angry. Then I believe that I have to somehow defend myself against them, to somehow attack them in return, to overcome and destroy them.

Positive judgments also involve fear. If I believe that my current happiness is caused by some person or thing outside my awareness, then I am still vulnerable, at least in my own mind. I believe that my well-being is dependent on forces outside my mind. At any moment, circumstances could change, the good things that I am so attached to could be taken away, or the person who is making me so happy could leave me or even die. Something might be taken from me because I somehow deserve punishment, or it might be arbitrarily snatched away with no rhyme or reason. Thus, in the very midst of my positive judgment of someone or something, there is an element of fear. And with that element of fear is also a shadow of resentment—the resentment that my happiness is at the mercy of someone or something else.

In short, whenever I believe that my happiness or unhappiness is caused by something external to my mind, there will always be some degree of underlying fear and resentment in my life. Sometimes it may be almost subconscious, present only as a vague feeling of anxiety that seems to be at the very edge of every experience. It might be more obvious in the form of worry or frustration or anger or hatred. But when I believe I am a victim at the mercy of external forces, I can never completely drop my guard. I can never completely allow myself to feel perfectly happy.

The Origin of Blame

The same mistake that gives rise to your unhappiness and suffering—ultimately, the mistaken belief in separation—also gives rise to your story of blame, which explains and justifies your experience of unhappiness and suffering. But since this story of blame is projected—interpretation parading as objective reality—you think that it is an actual experience of the world.

You believe that you are blaming another for your unhappiness *because* they really are guilty of threatening or harming you in some way—*because* they really have limited or destroyed your experience of well-being.

Any time you blame or condemn someone or something in the world for your misfortune and unhappiness, there are two levels of self-deception involved.

The fundamental self-deception is the mistaken idea that you are separate—separate from source and therefore limited, needy and vulnerable. These mistaken ideas of neediness and vulnerability are creatively translated as experiences of suffering and lack. And they are emotionally reflected as feelings of fear and unhappiness.

The second level of self-deception occurs when you make up and project a story that explains these feelings and experiences. This is a story of blame: a story of how the world and others have somehow attacked a vulnerable you and have caused your feelings of fear and unhappiness, and your experiences of suffering and lack. This story is creatively translated as your experience of others attacking you and harming you, or taking something from you. It is emotionally reflected as the unhappy feelings of fear and anger and hatred toward the people and events that have victimized you. (There are variations of this scenario. If you believe that someone else has been a victim, you might feel anger toward his victimizer. Or you might feel guilt or shame, if you believe that you yourself were his victimizer.)

Even though for the sake of clarity I have analyzed this process in terms of discrete levels and occurrences, all of these things come into being together. The initial choice to believe in separation is subconscious and not recognized as a "choice" or a "belief" at all. You think you *are* separate; you think that separateness is simply a given fact of existence. And that subconscious belief choice immediately gives rise to all the rest, which come into being together—including the experience of suffering and lack, the feelings of fear and unhappiness, the experience of being victimized by outside forces, and your feelings of anger toward the victimizer. You may believe and even experience that these elements came into being sequentially. For instance, you were feeling just fine, and then someone did something to you, and then you experienced suffering and lack, and then you felt afraid and unhappy, and then you were angry with the person who caused all of this. But from the perspective of one power and creative mind, this whole story (which seems to unfold over time, as stories do) came into being as the creative reflection of your mistaken idea of separation.

In other words, because you are unaware of the real cause of your experience of unhappiness and suffering, you subconsciously make up a substitute reason to explain it to yourself. This substitute reason is projected and then experienced as an event in the world outside yourself. This substitute reason is a story of how something outside of your mind is making your mind unhappy, and making it experience threat or suffering or loss. It could be a story of what someone is doing to you. Or a story about some unfavorable circumstance in your environment. Or a story about something that happened in the past. But in every case, the meaning of the story is that something outside of you is making you have unhappy feelings and experiences. Ironically, when you are upset about or angry at or afraid of those outside forces that seem to victimize you, what you are really upset at is your own projected story, your own interpretation. From the perspective of one power and creative mind, you are making up a story and then getting angry at that story. Put in these terms, doesn't it sound like a kind of insanity?

For instance, my unhappiness—arising from my mistaken belief in separation—could take the form of feeling insecure and unworthy. These thoughts and feelings will be creatively projected as my experience of others not supporting me enough, not respecting me enough and not encouraging me enough. It may even be projected as my experience of others actually criticizing and demeaning me. I will then believe that they are to blame for my feelings of insecurity and unworthiness—feelings which are causing me to be unhappy now. Therefore, I will feel anger or even hatred toward those unsupportive and critical people who have made me unhappy. In this example it is apparent that the story I am telling myself is almost the exact opposite of what is actually happening.

When I am in the midst of blaming my unhappiness on someone or something outside myself, I am effectively denying and hiding its real cause: my own belief in separation, in two powers. To projectively blame my unhappiness on something outside my awareness is to turn my attention away from the inward dimension of my mind, the only place where I could make any real change. Blaming something outside my mind for my unhappiness actively hides the solution and condemns me to continued unhappiness.

Unhappiness, projection, blame and attack form a vicious cycle. Everything I experience from a blaming state of mind will seem to justify my continued fear and anger. The more I attack those outside forces or try to defend myself against them, the more I affirm the reality of my vulnerability and victimhood. And my belief in my own vulnerability will be creatively translated as further experiences of being victimized. The way out of this cycle of blame and unhappiness is forgiveness.

Undoing Unforgiveness

We typically think that forgiveness means letting a guilty person off the hook. Letting him off the hook doesn't change the fact that he is guilty. You believe that he really did something wrong, did something to hurt you or another, did something to make you or another unhappy. But you are choosing to not hold it against him. You are choosing to overlook or deny the truth of his guilt—you are choosing to no longer remain actively angry with him even though he actually deserves your outrage. This kind of forgiveness implicitly affirms the real guilt of the person, even while it is letting go of condemnation.

From the perspective of these seven principles, however, the guilt was never true in the first place. On the one hand, there is only the power of love, so there is no real power that threatens or attacks our well-being. On the other hand, mind co-creates its own experience and can never be victimized by outside forces. So from this perspective, forgiveness is not a matter of overlooking or denying the truth. In fact, it is rather a choice to be completely truthful with yourself and the world. Forgiveness means simply letting go of the *mistaken thought* that your well-being and happiness can be affected by anything external to your awareness. To forgive another means to release him *in your own mind* from the *mistaken* thought that he is causing (or has caused, or could cause) your feelings of happiness or unhappiness, or that he is causing (or has caused, or could cause) your experiences of well-being or un-well-being.

Rather than thinking of forgiveness as something that you do, it can be helpful to think of it as the *undoing of unforgiveness*. Only when we are blaming someone for something do we need to forgive him. And as we have seen, to blame someone involves actively maintaining two levels of self-deception. Forgiveness is essentially the undoing or stopping of that on-going process of self-deception. And it is *self*-deception, for we are doing it to ourselves. There is no power out there that is trying to actively cloud our minds against our will. Only we can deceive ourselves, and only we can undo or stop it. Forgiveness is the exact opposite of overlooking or denying the truth. It is, in fact, the undoing of the obstacles we are maintaining in our minds that prevent us from knowing the truth. Our primary reason to forgive another is for *our own sakes*—we ourselves benefit from our own forgiveness. Forgiveness is an essential step (perhaps *the* essential step) on our journey to self-awareness and happiness.

Forgiveness is necessary only from within the context of blame, only from within the context of already projecting mistaken ideas about ourselves and others. And these ideas are being creatively translated into illusory experiences of guilt and suffering which block our ability to experience love. Forgiveness means letting go of our projected thoughts of guilt and victimhood and *extending* healing thoughts of innocence and invulnerability. Ultimately, forgiveness means letting go of our projected thoughts of separation and two powers, and *extending* the healing thought of one power. It's not enough to merely deny something—we need to replace our mistaken thoughts with more truthful thoughts. In more general terms, *extension is how we wake up from projection*. The real purpose of these seven principles is to offer thoughts that we can extend to help us undo the unhappiness and suffering made by the pervasive and taken-for-granted beliefs we have been projecting for most of our lives. The only truth and value of these principles is the extent to which they allow you to awaken to a deeper experience of love and joy.

Undoing unforgiveness means undoing every seemingly objective reason you use to make yourself unhappy; letting go of every seemingly valid argument you give yourself to feel angry or afraid, sad or frustrated; simply dropping every excuse you make to justify withholding unconditional love. Instead you choose to extend thoughts of innocence and invulnerability, well-being and perfect love.

When we first start to extend these healing thoughts, they will seem inconsistent with our current feelings and experiences. That is because our current feelings and experiences are the reflection of our previously projected thoughts of guilt and victimhood. So forgiveness will seem like a denial of truth to a mind which has lost itself in the ideas and experiences of separation and guilt and victimhood. But in truth, forgiveness is the way to find yourself again.

Don't Add the Idea of Victimhood

Forgiveness does not mean repressing or denying any unhappiness or suffering you may be feeling now. Be aware of everything that you are experiencing and feeling, including any upsetness or fear or suffering. Don't deny or repress anything; don't pretend that you feel anything different than you do. *Just don't add anything to your experience.* Don't add the idea or the story that what you are experiencing is being caused by some person or thing or circumstance that is external to your awareness and over which you have no control. *Forgiveness means letting go of the thought that your upsetness is being caused by something external to your awareness.*

If you are feeling upset with someone, for instance, be fully aware of your feeling of upsetness. But do not add the thought that it is being caused by her. If you feel unpeaceful with some situation, be fully aware of your feeling of unpeace. But do not add the thought that it is being caused by something external to your mind. If you are feeling upset with something from the past, be fully aware of your feelings of anger or sadness. But do not add the thought that these feelings are being caused by some past event that is, by definition, external to the now. Or if you are feeling upset about something in the future, be fully aware of your feeling of worry or anxiety. But do not add the thought that it is being caused by some possible future event that is, by definition, external to the now. And if you are feeling sick or un-well, be fully aware of that feeling. But do not add the thought that your feeling of un-wellness is being caused by something outside your mind.

In short, *do not add the thought of victimhood to your experience.*

In every case, choose to believe—choose to deliberately and consciously *extend* the interpretation—that your upsetness is somehow arising from and being caused by something in your own mind now. But because your mind does not wish to take responsibility for the upsetness, it has displaced the cause to something external. It has translated that upsetness into feeling victimized by external circumstances, by other things and people, by the past, or perhaps even by your own body in the form of sickness or pain or deterioration.

Note that this is not a question of whether or not an event "really" happened or not, whether someone "really" said or did a certain thing or not, or whether your medical report from the lab is "accurate" or not. Rather it is simply taking responsibility for your current experience of upsetness or suffering. It is your conscious acknowledgement that blaming something outside your mind for your unhappiness is only your own projection.

How you experience another person is always a reflection of your *thoughts* about her. Any time you are upset at another, you are really upset at your own projected interpretation of her. Likewise, the past and the future exist in your awareness simply as your *thoughts* about the past or the future, as memories or anticipations you are having *now*. When you are upset about the past or the future, you are really upset about your own *thoughts* about them *now*. Forgiveness is simply letting go of the *thought* that your present upsetness is the fault of someone or something outside your mind now.

It is important to understand that forgiveness does not mean denying that there are "others" in your life—others with whom you relate and interact, and to whom you can extend love and kindness. As we noted earlier, you are, at least in your current level of consciousness, in a relational kind of self-awareness. Your mind is aware of itself in the form of a you-in-a-world, a you-relating-to-others. But the *meaning and value* of that "you" and those others is always a reflection of the thoughts that you have projected or extended, always something that your own mind has added to your experience. Your *experience* of both the "you" character and the "others" is an expression of your creative mind. Forgiveness means simply letting go of the *thought* that those other people and things can cause your mind to feel happy or unhappy, peaceful or unpeaceful, loving or afraid, well or un-well.

Forgiveness Is Freedom

When I believe that I am separate from source, that belief will be reflected as the experience that I am separate from the world. I will experience myself as needy and vulnerable, and I will believe an external world of others is the cause of my feelings of lack and limitation. I will experience myself as a victim, and the world and others as my victimizers. I will also feel some sense of guilt whenever I think I am victimizing others.

When I am lost in this thought system, I will see others only relative to my imagined needs and lacks, only relative to what I can get from them, or what they can take from me. I will see them only as enemies or temporary allies in my on-going conflict and competition with others. And I will also see myself only in terms of this dynamic of taking and being taken from. Even the closest and strongest love relationships in my life, such as deep friendships and marriage and parenting, can harbor underlying beliefs in lack and need, which will surface as feelings of hurt and anger, disappointment and shame.

If you think of forgiveness as "letting someone off the hook," you believe that you are doing someone else a favor by forgiving them. After all, they are really guilty and deserve your judgment and condemnation. You are, however, magnanimously releasing them from punishment, while nevertheless maintaining your belief in their "real" guilt. In this version of forgiveness, you believe that you are doing someone else a favor by forgiving them. And even if you may later get a reward for this noble gesture, in the short run it is a kind of a sacrifice in which you give up your "right" to judge and condemn and perhaps to get even.

When you shift your understanding to a thought system based on the principles of one power and creative mind, you realize that *you* are one of the primary beneficiaries of your forgiveness. You are releasing yourself and others *in your own mind* from the *thoughts* of separation, limitation, victimhood and guilt. You are freeing *your own mind* from a self-made mental prison in which you experience others as potentially fearful and threatening enemies; you experience yourself as a frightened, needy victim; you experience your relationships only in terms of getting and taking; you experience your life as an on-going drama of conflict and suffering and lack. You are freeing *your own awareness* for the very possibility of experiencing the wholeness and creativity, the innocence and invulnerability, of yourself and others.

When you (in your own awareness) release another from his past—that is, from your current *story* of his past—you at the same time release yourself. When you release another from your *thought* of his guilt, you release yourself from your *thought* that you are a separate limited being who could have been scarred or wounded by external events. And simultaneously you release yourself from the *thought* that you are, or could be, the cause of another's hurt and suffering. You also release yourself from your *thought* that you are at the mercy of some linear causal chain of events that you call the "past."

In one of Jerry and Esther Hicks' recordings, Abraham pointed out that when you blame another or criticize his mistakes, *regardless* of whether your blame and criticisms are "accurate" or not, you are hurting *yourself.* You are reinforcing a belief system of separation, guilt, victimhood and struggle in your own mind, and thus are confining your own awareness to the perception of suffering, disappointment and lack.

Every negative criticism of another, *regardless* of whether it is accurate or not (and in truth, it is always just a projection), is focusing your attention on what you do not like. Your judgment and criticism and anger restrict your own mind's ability to feel love and joy now. They also effectively restrict your mind from manifesting the on-going creative flow of source toward ever-expanding well-being—focusing on what you do not like only brings more of it into your life experience. In short, your current negative judgmental thoughts make you unhappy now and continue to generate further unhappy feelings and experiences.

Conversely, when you focus on what you can appreciate about another, *regardless* of whether they seem to "deserve" your appreciation or not (and in their truth as be-ings of source, they always deserve it), you are benefiting *yourself.* Your praise and appreciation open your mind to feel love and joy now. Plus, your positive and happy thoughts allow your mind to more clearly and fully express the pure positive energy of source—focusing on what you like and appreciate in the world co-creates more of it in your experience. In short, your appreciation allows you to feel happy now and to continue to co-create further happy feelings and experiences.

Once again, this approach of focusing just on the positive would be "one-sided" only if both the light and the darkness were equally real. But if only the light is real, and the darkness is merely the temporary hiddenness of the light, then focusing only on the light is the best and most effective way to allow your mind to more fully see the truth.

This is not about denying or repressing your experiences of darkness and negativity. It is rather a matter of re-interpreting those experiences—seeing them as your own feedback signal guiding you to change the limiting beliefs that are casting shadows into your mind and blocking your awareness of the light.

The thoughts that you extend forth to the world are reflected back as your experiences of the world. The quality of your state of mind is reflected back as the quality of your experience. If you give appreciation and love you will receive appreciation and love. You reap exactly what you sow. Again, this is not a matter of punishment or reward—your experiences are simply the creative reflections of your thoughts.

As *creative* mind, your well-being and happiness are not dependent on any outside forces. You co-create your own experience of well-being, both by allowing it to freely manifest through you, and by giving the creative potential for well-being the form and shape of your own particular creative desires. The degree of manifestation of well-being in your life experience is wholly up to you. Your happiness is an inside job and is invulnerable to the world.

Likewise, the love and appreciation that you happily extend to the world is invulnerable to circumstances and to others' words and behavior. In this sense, forgiveness could be understood as letting go of all of your reasons to not appreciate and love, all of your reasons to not be happy now.

When you relate to another with unconditional love and unconditional happiness, you are demonstrating to her both your invulnerability and her innocence. You are effectively teaching her a new paradigm of thought by living that model yourself. In freeing yourself and others in your own mind from the thought-prison of limitation and guilt, you implicitly help them to free themselves in their minds. Your very being provides an example of wholeness and happiness, of creativity and invulnerability. Plus, your vision of their truth and their potential helps to awaken them to becoming more aware of it themselves.

Forgiveness is freedom. In forgiving, we free ourselves and others from the illusion that unhappiness, guilt, fear, anger and suffering are inevitable. We free ourselves and others to discover the possibility of co-creating a life experience of perfect happiness, perfect peace and unconditional love—of co-creating the manifestation of our deepest and truest desires.

Practicing the Principle of
Forgiveness Is Freedom

Wayne Dyer pointed out that when you squeeze an orange you get orange juice. You get orange juice *because the orange juice was in the orange.* It makes no difference who does the squeezing, or what they use to squeeze the orange. Orange juice comes out because there was orange juice in the orange. Likewise when (my interpretation of) another's words or actions trigger feelings of insecurity or fear or anger in me, it is only because those feelings were already in me. What comes out when you are squeezed is never the fault of the squeezer. It is only the explicit expression of what was already implicit within your mind.

What in your life do you feel upset about now? Who or what do you hold responsible for any negative feelings that you are experiencing now? Remind yourself that the upsetness was already in you before you were "squeezed." Release the other person from the mistaken thought that they caused your upsetness. How do you feel now?

In conjunction with this practice, I would also suggest a very simple exercise from *A Course in Miracles.* Whenever you are feeling unhappy, remind yourself, "I could feel peace instead of this."

Whenever you feel upset about something or someone external to you, think of it as some unease in your own mind that is being creatively translated into the experience of someone doing something "to" you. Something internal is being projected in the form of blame. Do not deny the upsetness that you feel. *Just don't add anything*—don't add the *thought* that it is being caused by something external to your mind.

When you are upset about something that happened in the past, think of it as some unease in your own mind that is being creatively translated into the memory of a past event that somehow wounded or limited you. Again, something internal is being projected in the form of blame. Do not deny the upsetness that you feel. *Just don't add anything*—don't add the *thought* that it is being caused by something external to your mind now.

When you feel pain or sickness, think of it as some unease in your own mind that is being creatively translated into the form of the experience of physical discomfort being caused by something (i.e., your body) external to your mind. Once again, something internal is being projected in the form of blame. Do not deny the discomfort that you feel. *Just don't add anything*—don't add the *thought* that it is being caused by a body-thing that is external to your mind.

This is an exercise in deliberately re-interpreting your experience. The issue here is not whether so-and-so "really" did that thing, nor whether some past event "really" happened, nor whether the medical tests are "really" correct or not. For now, suspend those kinds of questions. Deliberately think of your experience of "something external making you suffer" as simply the creative projection of some unease within your own mind. Think of it as similar to the way in which some unease in your subconscious mind might express itself as a sleeping dream of victimhood and suffering. The purpose of this whole practice is to help you to realize that externality and blame are *thoughts* rather than simply given facts.

Remember, however, that this exercise is not about blaming yourself for your experiences of suffering. The purpose of this exercise is rather to discover how your experience changes when you let go of the *thought* that something external to you is the cause of your upsetness.

3 When you blame another or criticize his mistakes, *regardless* of whether your blame and criticisms are accurate or not, you are hurting *yourself.* When you praise or appreciate another, *regardless* of whether she "deserves" your praise and appreciation or not, you are benefiting *yourself.*

Consider any person from the previous two exercises that you had blamed for your upsetness. Ask yourself, "What could I appreciate about that person now?" Don't stop asking until you have at least one good answer—one that you know is good because it brings you a sense of peace and joy.

The next time you find yourself in the midst of blaming or criticizing another, see it as an *opportunity* to do *yourself* a favor and shift your awareness to appreciation. Ask yourself, "What could I appreciate about this person?" Again, don't stop asking until you have at least one good answer.

Love Is Being Yourself

Love is the creative process of self-awarely being your truth. It is the very essence of all true happiness in your life. Being loving is being happy, and being happy is being loving.

This book starts off by saying, "Happiness is the promise and the goal of life." Some of you may have asked at that point, "What about love? Isn't love the real promise and goal of life?" Sometimes we believe that we have to choose between love and happiness. We believe that love means sacrificing our own interests for the sake of helping others. From that perspective, the statement that "happiness is the promise and goal of life" might seem to promote mere selfishness and self-gratification. Here "self" would refer to the separate limited "you," the needy vulnerable "you," defined by a separative or two-power thought system.

In the thought system of these seven principles, however, love and happiness could never be opposed. Love and happiness are two aspects of the same thing: two aspects of self-awarely living your truth. Love is a state of being—ultimately, your state of being when you are truly being yourself—and happiness is the emotional reflection of that state of being.

To be Loving *is* to be Happy, and to be Happy *is* to be Loving

With regard to source, love can be thought of as the infinite eternal creative potential for ever-expanding well-being. With regard to ourselves, love is a state of being or a state of mind, a way we relate to ourselves and the world. It is not a particular thing that we "do," and it is not romantic or possessive love.

Rather, it is the state of mind of unconditionally extending forth good will. This is the state of mind that most clearly and fully expresses the truth of source.

The state of mind of love is creatively expressed as experiences of happiness and well-being, and feelings of peace and joy. In being loving—that is, in extending perfect happiness to others—we ourselves are happy, and we co-create the manifestation of our truest desires. In short, *to be loving is to be happy, and to be happy is to be loving.*

Fear, however, is a state of mind that withholds love. A fearful mind believes that it withholds love because the world is unlovable. But in truth, the unlovableness that you perceive in the world is simply a reflection of the unloving quality of your awareness. The quality or tone of your awareness determines the quality of what you perceive (and not vice versa). You, and *only you*, can control the quality of your own awareness. The self-reinforcing cycle of withholding love and seeing the world as unlovable grows out of the un-source-like thoughts of separation, guilt and victimhood—thoughts which actively restrict your experience of happiness and well-being. Both "being unloving" and "being unhappy" are reflections of the same underlying core beliefs. *To be unloving is to be unhappy, and to be unhappy is to be unloving.*

Love is an inclusive state of mind that embraces all others as expressions of its own self. Fear, however, is an exclusive state of mind that reacts against what it believes to be separate from itself—that is, what it has projectively interpreted as separate from itself. From the perspective of these seven principles, fear is the denial of love—fearing *is* not-loving.

But in an absolute sense, to say that fear is the "opposite" of love would be misleading. According to the principle of one power, there *is* only love, and beyond love there is nothing. As it says in the first page of *A Course in Miracles*, "The opposite of love is fear, but what is all-encompassing can have no opposite.... Nothing real can be threatened. Nothing unreal exists. Herein lies the peace of God."

From the perspective of one power, the experience of separation is only a reflection of our denial of wholeness, only a self-imposed restriction of our ability to be aware of wholeness. In this sense, separation is not the absence of wholeness, since there *is* only the wholeness of one power. The experience of separation is only the *illusion* of the absence of wholeness. Likewise, fear is not really the absence of love, since there is only love and beyond love there is nothing. *Fear is only the **illusion** of the absence of love.*

But even though fear (or anger or hatred) is only illusory in an absolute sense, it can seem very real for us in our current state of mind. If we lived in the awareness of perfect oneness and love, we would already be perfectly happy all of the time, and there would be no need for any principles or practices of happiness. There would be no need to talk about the illusory nature of fear, or undoing the limiting beliefs that restrict our awareness of love. There would be no need to actively cultivate a more loving relationship with ourselves and others and the world.

When we are in the illusion of separation and fear, however, it can be very valuable to understand how our own thoughts and beliefs can make the experience of a fearful and hateful world. Intellectually understanding that fear is an illusion doesn't make it automatically disappear from our lives. But we do realize that we no longer need to feel controlled by it, as if it were some real power in itself.

Likewise, it can be very valuable to understand how *being* loving is an essential part of our creative role in our own happiness. Any other way of relating to the world only reinforces the illusion of separation and vulnerability, and thus continues to make unhappiness. When we restrict the love we extend, we also restrict our own minds from manifesting happiness and well-being in our own experience.

You Are Your Relationships

We find ourselves in the kind or level of self-awareness called perception. In perception, self-awareness takes the form of a you-in-a-world, a "you" interacting with some "other" person or thing. Your self-awareness exists as a story of the relationship between that "you" character and someone or something else. This "someone or something else" can include other people, things and circumstances, your environment, the world at large, or even God. In this sense, you (that is, your mind or awareness) *are* your relationships.

Your "relationship" with the world and others essentially means how you *think about* the relationship between you and them. How you think about your relationship with others defines both what you are and what they are—defines how you and they exist in your awareness. Your words and your behavior toward others can also, of course, be an important part of your day-to-day relating to others. But ultimately it is how you think about others that is the foundation of your relationship with them. Your words and actions are simply reflections and expressions of your thoughts.

There are fundamentally two ways of thinking about your relationship with others. You can think of the other as separate from you with his own separate will and agenda, and therefore as a potential threat to you. Then you experience your relationship with the other as an on-going struggle and competition. Or, you can think of yourself and the other as two creative expressions of a shared source of love. Then you will experience your relationship with the other as two creative minds joyfully co-creating life experiences, both individually and in concert with one another.

When you project separation and blame, you will think of your relationship with others in terms of fear and attack. Because you relate to others with fear, you will experience them as fearful enemies. When you extend love, however, you will think of your relationship with others in terms of love and oneness. Because you relate to them with love, you will experience them as lovable friends.

As we have discussed above, the belief that you are separate (from source, from others, from life, from the universe, from God) gives rise to fear. All negative thoughts and emotions are expressions of fear. All negative experiences are the reflections of negative thoughts and emotions. Thus the underlying cause of all unhappiness and every unhappy experience is the belief that you are separate.

Within this context of fear and attack, the word "love" comes to mean a kind of barter with others. In the midst of the on-going war of you versus everyone else, you make temporary alliances—alliances against common enemies, or alliances for refuge from the constant stress of conflict and competition. This kind of love is always conditional love, a "giving to get." You sacrifice a little of your time and energy in order to get something in return, something you believe will make you happy. These alliances are ultimately only temporary, since your needs and others' needs are ever-changing. So you can never fully extend love. You always have to keep your guard up, always have to be ready for possible change or betrayal.

It is very important to note that this bartering kind of "love" is not really love at all. When seen in its truth, it is fundamentally a manipulation of the other to get something from him. But within separation awareness, this is as good as a relationship can be. The problem is that when you believe that this is what love means, you effectively blind yourself to experiencing any deeper and truer form of love. You blind yourself to the very possibility of extending or experiencing perfect or unconditional love.

The alternative way of relating to others is thinking of yourself and others as extensions of a common shared source of perfect love. In effect, you think of all of the others in your life as your other selves, as other expressions of the one creative power for well-being. This way of thinking about and seeing others is reflected as unconditional love for all of life.

When you extend only love to others, you experience a lovable world *because* you are thinking loving thoughts, *because* you are relating to others with love. At this stage in our journey, we tend to shift back and forth between believing in one power and believing in two powers. How we think and feel about the personal relationships in our lives reflects this on-going shifting back and forth between a loving and a fearful state of mind. For instance, we might feel unconditional love for our spouse in one moment and be angry and judgmental in the next. From the perspective of these seven principles, any angry or judgmental thought is an opportunity to forgive and to once again extend love.

When you know you are *creative* mind, you are free to extend perfect or unconditional love. You are an individualized expression of the infinite extending-forth of love, and there is no limit to its power to *create* love. Love is never a sacrifice, nor is it a moral obligation. You never have to withhold love in any way, as if you were doling it out from a limited supply. By extending-forth love, you are allowing your mind to express and manifest and experience the infinite love of source.

In this state of mind, you know that your own happiness and well-being are the effect of your co-creative collaboration with source. There is nothing outside your awareness that can threaten or harm your well-being. So there is never any reason to withhold love or to make your love conditional in any way. In fact, you realize that *it is precisely by withholding love that you restrict your own experience of happiness and well-being.* So not only do you not have any reason to withhold love, but you indeed have every reason to extend perfect and unconditional love all of the time.

In perception consciousness, you become aware of what you are projecting or extending by observing what you are perceiving. You become aware of your thoughts and your state of mind by observing their creative experiential reflections. You know how you are relating to others by how you perceive them and how you feel about them. Your experience of someone or something as lovable is a reflection of your loving thoughts. Happy experiences are the witnesses to your own extending-forth of love.

Happiness Is Self-Awarely Being Yourself

Source is pure positive energy, pure benevolence. In short, source *is* love. Source is not a something that loves. Source *is* love, the very Being of love. It belongs to the nature of source to creatively expand—love expresses itself as lov-ing. Source is the very loving-ness, the infinite eternal loving extension of love itself. Source *is* love loving unconditionally, pure benevolence freely and creatively extending and offering well-being.

Source expresses its creativity as creative mind, which is a self-aware process of extending love and co-creating experience. At the absolute level of source, there is no "other," because beyond source there is nothing. At that level, love simply exists as an eternal extending-forth—not extending forth "to" anything, but just an eternal creative expanding-ness. But we are currently in the kind of self-awareness called perception, in which creative mind exists as a relationship between a "you" and an "other." In this kind of self-awarness, you express the love that is your essence by extending forth love from you and the other—in other words, you express love by loving others.

So in perception awareness, you most fully express your truth as your creative extending-forth of unconditional love to all, including yourself. This *is* your truth whether you are aware of it or not. You *are* an extension of source energy, and source energy is the creative extension of love. And since source is the only power, this is the *only* truth of your mind.

When you are aware of your truth, you self-awarely relate to others with unconditional love. This way of relating is emotionally reflected as feelings of joy. *Happiness is the emotional reflection of self-awarely being who you truly are.* This "who" that you truly are is not a thing, but an ever-evolving, creatively-expanding process of lovingly becoming. Your being *is* your eternal creative becoming.

Un-self-awareness will always take the form of seeming to be aware of some substitute idea of "you" that you have made up. I say "seeming" to be aware, since there really isn't some other untrue "you" that you could actually be aware of. You are only aware of an image or illusion of an untrue idea of yourself.

It is impossible to "not be yourself" in any absolute sense—you *are* an extension of source, and there is no power that can change that truth. But if you have a false conception of yourself, then you can *imagine* that you are something different than what you truly are. And those meaningless thoughts will be creatively translated into illusory experiences of this alternate "you." Your meaningless thoughts of your own separation, limitation and victimhood will be creatively translated into experiences of a limited and vulnerable "you" enmeshed in a world of suffering and lack, a world of fearful and hateful others who threaten and harm that you.

This substitute idea of yourself is the cause of all of the fear you experience, and thus of all of your negative unloving emotions. *Unhappiness is the emotional reflection of the **illusion** of not being yourself*—the emotional reflection of your meaningless thoughts about being a separate limited "you." These thoughts not only make you unhappy when you are thinking them, but they will be creatively translated into negative and unhappy life experiences. All of your unhappy experiences are ultimately the reflections of your untrue thoughts about yourself and your relationship to source.

You know that you are in an illusory and un-self-aware state of mind whenever you are feeling unhappy. This unhappiness usually takes some form of feeling critical or judgmental of yourself or others—some form of being unloving, some form of feeling unworthy, angry, afraid or hateful. Consciously or subconsciously you will tend to look for what is wrong in the world, to look for aspects and qualities of others that you can criticize. And you will seem to find what you are looking for, even when what you are looking for isn't real. You will know that you are in a separation state of mind when you find yourself experiencing an unlovable world, a world of bad and fearful things, a world of wrong and hateful people (including yourself).

In this context, *forgiveness means letting go of all of those projected thoughts that are keeping you un-self-aware.* Said another way, *forgiveness means letting go of every thought that would make you withhold love*—undoing all of the stories that you have made up to rationalize and justify limiting the love that you extend to others. Since happiness is the emotional reflection of self-awarely being yourself or extending love, *forgiveness means undoing those thoughts that are making you unhappy. A primary beneficiary of your forgiveness is yourself,* since the more love you extend, the more love and happiness and well-being you experience.

Gratitude and Appreciation

Once you have undone the thoughts that you have been using to make yourself unhappy, you are in a position to shift your thoughts and your focus to what feels more positive and more lovable to you. Once you have suspended your judgment and condemnation, you can begin to actively shift your focus to *appreciation.* To deliberately appreciate or be grateful means to *actively look for what is lovable in your experience,* to actively look for those things and qualities in your experience that you like and feel good about. As always, you will tend to find what you look for, since your experiences creatively reflect your thoughts and your focus of attention. The more that you think about and look for the lovable, the more you find it and the happier you feel.

Appreciation or gratitude is a primary way to co-create happiness and happy experiences in your life—a primary way to allow your mind to manifest the pure positive energy of source in your feelings and your life experience. Forgiveness deliberately lets go of those thoughts that are restricting your mind's ability to manifest and experience love's will. *Appreciation is a way of proactively opening your mind to the experience of well-being and happiness.*

As we discussed earlier, when you appreciate or praise another, *regardless* of whether she seems to "deserve" your praise and appreciation or not, you are benefiting *yourself.* In focusing on and affirming the positive in life, you are effectively allowing your awareness to more clearly express and experience the pure positive energy of source.

Your focus on the positive and the lovable in another not only benefits you, but it can help her to see her own creative potential for love and joy more clearly. Your focus helps her to release herself from her own fearful mental prison of guilt and conflict, and to shift her own attention to thoughts that allow her mind to more fully express source in her experience. Your appreciation not only opens you to experiencing more happiness in your life, but it is the primary way that you help others open themselves to experience more happiness in their lives.

Self-Awarely Extending Love

Consciously extending love is the final step in the process of undoing the mental prison of unhappiness and moving into the freedom to deliberately co-create true happiness.

Forgiveness is the first step, and it frees your mind from the illusory need to defend itself against external forces that seem to you to threaten your happiness. It frees you from your own projected stories of guilt and attack that keep you in a mental prison of fear.

Gratitude or appreciation is an intermediate step that focuses on and uncovers the lovable, and thus makes it easier to extend love—an intermediate step that helps to shift you from a fearful way of relating to the world to a loving way of relating.

Ultimately, however, *your goal is to be love*—to *self-awarely* be what you already eternally are, by consciously and deliberately extending forth unconditional love.

The very nature of love is to eternally extend forth love. Source *is* love—the very being of source is the eternal extending-forth of love. You, in your essence, are an individualized expression of this extending-forth. You self-awarely express your nature—you are self-awarely your truth—by consciously extending forth love.

So we can think of the process of waking up from un-self-awareness in terms of these three steps. First, forgiveness undoes your illusory thoughts about yourself and allows you to think truer thoughts. It opens you to be more fully and clearly who you (already and eternally) are. Then gratitude is like priming the pump, helping you shift from the illusion of not being who you are, to actively and self-awarely being who you are. And finally, *being loving is self-awarely being who you are.*

As we said above, happiness is the emotional reflection of self-awarely being who you are, the reflection of self-awarely extending unconditional love to all beings. Another way to say this is that *happiness is how you feel when you are no longer imagining that you are not who you are.* Happiness is how you feel when you are no longer subconsciously making yourself unhappy; when you are no longer making and living the unhappy illusion of not being yourself; when you are no longer withholding love.

It is important to remember that all love is ultimately the love of source. It is the love of source in two senses. First, it is the love of source in the sense that it is source that is doing the loving. Or more precisely, it is source that is *being* the loving. When you are self-awarely living your truth, the love you are expressing and extending does not come from some limited supply "in you" (as if there were some separate you that could have its own supply). The love you extend forth is an expression of the infinite eternal creative potential for well-being— an expression of source itself. Second, all love is the love of source in the sense that source is the object of your love. In perception awareness, your mind is aware of itself in the form of a "you" relating to an "other," and "you" express your truth by unconditionally extending forth love "to" the "other." But ultimately, source is the only reality that could either interact with or be interacted with. *Every relationship is ultimately one expression of source relating to another expression of source. All love is ultimately source loving itself.* The love that your mind extends to another is one expression of your truth extending love to another expression of your truth—the deeper Self of your mind expressing Its love for Itself.

Ways of Extending Love

Source is love, the infinite eternal creative extending-forth of well-being. There are several aspects of this extending-forth. As a being of source, you must express love in *all* of these ways to fully live your truth.

When you are in a oneness kind of consciousness, such as you might experience in deep meditation, you would simply be a pure creative extending-forth of well-being, a pure creative outpouring of love. There would be no "you" and no "other"— you would simply *be* love loving.

When you are in perception consciousness, the extending-forth of love exists as the extending-forth of love "to" all beings. The essence of this extending-forth of love is your inner vision of the eternal truth of the other person as a creative be-ing of love, coupled with the loving wish that he become fully self-aware of his truth—the loving wish that he experience perfect peace and joy and well-being in every area of his life, in whatever form would be most appropriate for him.

Your extending-forth of love also includes extending love to yourself. This can take the form of allowing yourself to have and manifest your desires. Your desires are your own thoughts of what particular kinds of experiences would best symbolize well-being for you, would be most joyful for you. Often we believe that our own desires are somehow in conflict with being truly loving—as if love means altruistic self-sacrifice, and personal desires are purely selfish. But within perception consciousness, the *universal* and unconditional love of source takes the form of extending-forth of love to *all* beings, which necessarily includes extending forth love and goodwill to yourself. From the perspective of one power, however, your "self" is not understood as a *separate* being, and self-love is not understood as loving yourself instead of or at the expense of others. Your self is simply one expression of creative mind, one expression of source. And creating and manifesting your desires—i.e., creating your true desires and allowing them to become manifest in your awareness—is one way that you express source, the infinite creative extending-forth of well-being that is the truth of all life.

As an expression of creative mind, you exist simultaneously in *all* of these ways, from pure oneness consciousness, to relating to others, to relating to your own self. To fully and self-awarely live your truth means to express love in *all* of these ways. Living your truth as a creative being of unconditional and universal love includes the whole spectrum, from the being of pure love, to the selfless extension of love to others, to the creation and manifestation of your heart's desires. In the oneness of your being, which is a reflection of the oneness of source, *all* these forms exist as an integral whole. To condemn or deny any form would be to deny one integral aspect of the whole, and thus to deny the whole itself. To deny or repress any expression of love, including your own desires, would be to hide your own true happiness from yourself. Happiness is the emotional reflection of self-awarely and fully living your truth.

Any thought that limits my universal and unconditional extending-forth of love limits my self-aware expression of my truth. Any thought that I or others are unworthy or incapable of giving and receiving perfect love will prevent me in my own mind from fully and deliberately expressing my truth. This will limit both my own happiness and what I could contribute to the happiness of others.

*Your potential to joyfully extend perfect love **is** your essence, and it is the **only** truth and power within you.* You can deny it and hide it from your awareness, but you cannot extinguish it. As soon as you stop actively hiding it, it will spontaneously and necessarily reveal and express itself, for beyond this power there is nothing real at all. *In every moment, your purpose*—how you are truly yourself, how you fulfill your role in your own happiness and in the happiness of the world—*is to be happy and to extend love now.*

Practicing the Principle of
Love Is Being Yourself

Gratitude or appreciation is an intentional focus on the positive, on what you already perceive as good. When you appreciate someone, you are focusing on her source-like qualities. According to the principle of one power, source is the *only* truth and reality of her. Anything else that you seem to see, anything that you perceive as un-source-like in any way, is ultimately only your own mistaken projection.

Moreover, when you appreciate another, you are expressing the source-like truth of yourself, as a be-ing of love.

Understood in this way, *gratitude is the practice of being and seeing only the truth—in the belief that if you practice being and seeing only the truth, you will eventually be and see only the truth. And when you are being and seeing only the truth, you will feel only gratitude.*

Today, practice being grateful for everything you possibly can. Actively look for things and qualities to appreciate. Whenever it is appropriate, you might even choose to openly express your gratitude to others. But in your mind, direct your gratitude to source itself. Appreciate the lovable things and qualities you experience not so much as separate realities in themselves but rather as expressions of source, of the infinite creative potential for well-being—expressions which your own appreciation is allowing you to see clearly. Be grateful not so much for the particular form, but for the unchanging, ever-present love that is eternally expressing itself in your experience as your consciousness of these ever-changing forms of well-being.

And also be grateful for the fact that you can recognize and appreciate these gifts of source, because your ability to do so fills your life experience with beauty and grace.

It can be very helpful to keep a gratitude journal to reinforce the process of appreciation. The more you practice extending thoughts of appreciation, the more it will become your habitual way of relating to the world. Plus, whenever you are temporarily lost in negative thoughts, looking at your journal can help you remember your way back to love and happiness.

2 Who in your life do you feel critical of now? Make a list and address them one by one. Every criticism is a withholding of love, which is ultimately a withholding of your own experience of well-being. The next time you find yourself in the midst of blaming or criticizing another, see it as an *opportunity* to do *yourself* a favor and shift your awareness to love. Extend love to the other, regardless of whether you think they "deserve" it or not. *Become* the extending-forth of unconditional love.

3 This is a meditation for deeper self-awareness. Set aside a quiet time without distractions. Become aware of yourself as a be-ing of love now on all levels: the eternal expansion of love at the level of the oneness of Being; extending forth unconditional love to others at the level of relationships in the world; and extending forth of unconditional love to yourself.

What mental obstacles do you encounter when you try to shift your awareness to love? How and why are you withholding love now? What judgments of others or of yourself are holding you back? Let go of those judgmental thoughts now. *Become* love.

Afterwards take some time to write down whatever you discovered about yourself in the course of this exercise.

CHOOSING
HAPPINESS NOW

*In your truth, you **are** the
realizing of love's will. You
realize love's will both by extending
thoughts of love and happiness, and
by experiencing love and happiness
in your life. Your role in fulfilling
your purpose is to choose love and
happiness **now.***

It has often been said that now is the only time you have, the only time you exist. Now is the only time you can be aware of anything. Now is the only time that you can feel anything. Now is the only time you can choose anything.

But how you *think about and understand* "the now" will determine, in large part, what you can feel and what you can experience. And even more importantly, it will determine how you try to change your experience when you feel unhappy or unpeaceful and even whether you believe it is possible to change it at all.

In this chapter, we will look at two fundamentally different ways of understanding the now.

The first way of understanding the now grows out of a separative or two-power way of thinking. It understands the now as one separate moment of *time*—one separate moment in an infinitely long linear sequence of separate moments that all exist external to you. In this way of thinking, you are "in time" and subject to the "laws of time." These laws determine what you are, what you experience, what you feel, and what is possible for you.

The second way of understanding the now grows out of a one-power thought system. It understands the now as an *eternal*—i.e., timeless—moment that is not "in time" at all. From this perspective, you in your deepest truth are not in time nor are you subject to the laws of time. Time and the laws of time are projections of creative mind. Mind does not exist in time—rather, the idea and experience of time exist within awareness. This is not to say that time is an individual subjective fantasy that exists only "in your head." As we discussed earlier, that individual "you" with its separate body and its separate consciousness is also only an idea within creative mind.

The Stories We Tell Ourselves

Perception always involves interpretation. You are telling yourself a story about what you are experiencing, giving it meaning, making sense of it for yourself. By the time you are aware of something as "something," you have already interpreted it—*perception is already interpreted experience*. Your story is always a story about something that *is already under way*, is already happening. To make sense of it, your story must include not only a description of what is happening, but also some explanation of how it came to be and some indication of where it is headed. So your interpretation always includes, at least implicitly, your stories about the "is" and the "already" and the "under way."

The two different ways of interpreting the now of perception are essentially two different kinds of stories about the "is" and the "already" and the "under way." The separative or two-power way of thinking interprets the "is" as the present moment of time, the "already" in terms of previous moments of time (the "past"), and the "under way" in terms of later moments of time (the "future").

The one-power way of thinking sees this whole of idea of external linear time as a projection of thought that is taking place in the now, a projected story about "previous moments" and "later moments" that exist external to (your story of) the "current moment."

Of course, the one-power way of thinking is telling its own story about the now, since perception necessarily involves interpretation and story-telling. And its story necessarily includes parts about the "is" and the "already" and the "under way." But the one-power way of thinking does not understand the "is" and the "already" and the "under way" as separate moments of time, but rather as interrelated aspects of the eternal dynamic of creation.

One way to understand the difference between these two perspectives is to look at their respective stories about the process of perception itself.

The separative or two-power way of thinking understands perception—i.e., tells itself a story about perception—as a process that is caused by an external world imprinting itself on a receptive consciousness. This receptive consciousness is encased within a body, and this body exists in an external world of bodies existing in space and time. Bodies and space and time all exist external to mind and independent of mind.

The one-power way of thinking understands perception as a process caused by the eternal dynamic of creative mind working in concert with source. From this perspective, "body" and "space" and "time" are all *interpretive thoughts* mind creates in order to make sense of its experience. These thoughts are not "wrong" in any way. Indeed these ideas can often be a useful way to interpret our experience. But if you think of them as external realities that somehow enslave and determine your mind, then you are effectively making yourself into a victim of your own projected thoughts.

Time as an External Linear Sequence

Again, for a separative or two-power way of thinking, the "is" and "already" and "under way" components of perception are understood in terms of external linear time. You think of time as a reality that exists external to your awareness. You believe that your brain and your perceiving consciousness are encased in your body, and your body exists "in" time. Thus your mind is also "in" time. You believe that the reason that you experience your life in temporal terms is *because* the external reality of time is causing you to have that kind of experience.

Thus you understand the "already" of your story to refer to the past—to previous moments of time. The "is "refers to the present—to the current moment of time in which experience is happening. The "under way" points toward the future—to later moments of time in which things either change or continue to be the same. All of these moments are strung together in an infinite linear sequence. These moments are all external to one another. The moments of the past are external to the now insofar as they have already happened. The events and possibilities inherent in the past moments "no longer exist" now in the present moment. Likewise, the things and events in the future moments "do not exist yet" in the present moment.

What happens in an earlier moment can determine or have an effect on what happens in a later moment. But what happens in a later moment cannot have a retroactive effect on a previous moment, because the previous moment has, after all, already happened. It is already a done deal, and nothing I do later can change what already happened. I cannot un-break the glass I dropped yesterday. I cannot un-say that spiteful thing I said yesterday or undo the hurt I caused another last week.

In this way of thinking, time is understood as a process of loss and limitation—the loss of innocence, the loss of love, the loss of possibilities for healing and happiness. In science, this is sometimes referred to as the law of entropy—life becomes progressively disorganized. Aging is understood as the progressive degeneration and disorganization of the body. Or more simply, life is considered to be a process of dying.

This way of looking at the world is not considered pessimistic at all—it is simply seeing things as they are. You can ignore the fact or repress it. Or you can resign yourself to it. Or you can use it to spur yourself on to pay more attention in every moment. Or you can choose to believe that there is another life that is "after" this one, "after" the dying is complete. This other life is eternal and unchanging, although you don't get to experience it until after you die in this life. But however you choose to respond, it is a simple fact, at least for this way of thinking, that life *is* a process of dying.

This way of thinking uses the events of time—including the ones that have already happened, the ones that are happening now, and the ones that are about to happen—as a way to explain how you feel now and whatever limitations you may believe you have now. The things that have already happened are external to the now. The things that are "coming your way" in the future are external to the now. For that matter, even the things that are presently happening "in the world" are external to your mind now. And all of these external forces and powers are making you have your current experiences and feelings.

In summary, for a separation way of thinking, the past exists as a dimension of loss that has caused the guilt and resentment and limitation you feel now. The future exists as a dimension of fear and further loss. Even if you have some things that you are looking forward to, it is all happening within the context of progressive loss and dying, within the context of eventually and inevitably losing *all* of your possibilities of this life. The now is always, at least to some extent, a moment of guilt and fear. Even in your moments of feeling good, there is an undercurrent of anxiety that everything could change in a heartbeat, and you could lose all of those qualities and relationships and circumstances and possessions that are "making" you happy now. In the midst of every moment of conditional happiness, there is a whisper of fear.

External Linear Time Understood as Projection

As we have already seen, negative or unhappy feelings and experiences are *intrinsic* to a separative way of thinking. When you believe that you are separate from the source and from everything else, you will feel cut off, limited, vulnerable and afraid. The only way such a state of experience can persist is if you are making it for yourself *subconsciously*, because you wouldn't consciously and deliberately continue to make yourself unhappy. At the conscious level, you tell yourself that outside forces beyond your control are causing your unhappy feelings and experiences. Projection and blame are an inherent part of a separation way of thinking.

Thus you look for external reasons for your unhappiness— something someone has done or said, some circumstance in your environment or something in your past. And you find what you are looking for. That means you succeed in making up and believing a story of blame, a story of how someone or something outside of your mind now is responsible for causing the unhappiness and un-well-being you are experiencing now.

Both "making yourself unhappy by thinking restricting thoughts" *and* "projecting the blame for that unhappiness onto the past and the future" come into being *simultaneously* as interrelated expressions of the same thought system.

You subconsciously make up a story that you are feeling upset or unhappy now *because* something outside the now has somehow harmed you (or another) in the past, or is threatening to harm you in the future. You tell yourself that you feel unhappy *because* something external to you is "making" you unhappy, "making" you feel afraid, anxious, wounded or angry. Even when you are feeling guilty for something that you yourself did, you are blaming your present feeling of guilt on a past event that is external to the now. In this context, it makes no difference whether or not a given event "really happened." What actually exists in the now is the story you are telling yourself about how this past event is *causing* you to feel unhappy now.

Earlier I said that projection is, by definition, a subconscious process. Of course, when you "project" blame, you are aware that you are blaming someone or something else outside yourself. But you are not aware that it is simply your interpretation. You believe that something outside yourself "really" is at fault and that you are blaming it *because* of what it did to you.

For instance, if you are feeling inadequate or guilty now, the "past" is the story you tell yourself of how you came to be this way—a story that explains and justifies your current unhappiness. You tell yourself that you cannot possibly be happy now *because* of that awful thing that happened to you in your past or that awful thing you yourself did in the past. From the perspective of separation awareness, the bad event of the past occurred *before* you felt bad, and it *caused* you to feel bad—or more to the point, it *is causing* you to feel bad now.

Likewise, if you are feeling afraid or anxious, you projectively imagine a threatening future that explains and justifies your present fear. You tell yourself that you are afraid now *because* you are facing a threatening future.

For a one-power way of thinking, the past and the future—at least insofar as they exist in your own experience—are just *thoughts* you are thinking in the *now*, memories and anticipations that you are entertaining in the now. When the past or the future seems to "weigh on" your mind now, it is only because you are thinking heavy, weighty thoughts about them *now*.

From this perspective, your current sense of limitation or guilt or unhappiness is the reason that you subconsciously make up and project a story of a past of guilt and loss. Likewise, your current sense of limitation and fear and anxiety is the reason that you subconsciously make up and project a story of a future of possible (or even certain) threat and loss.

For the one-power way of thinking, it is ultimately the thoughts that you are thinking *now* that are causing *both* your unhappy feelings and experiences now, *and* your projection of blame to explain and justify your sense of unhappiness and limitation. In terms of the "already-now-under-way" structure of perception, the separative view interprets the "now" as limited and vulnerable, the "already" as a past of loss that has caused it, and the "under way" as a further extension of loss and dying.

From the perspective of one power and creative mind, your whole sense of your limitation and lack and guilt is only an illusion. In your truth, you are neither lacking nor guilty, not now and not ever. So there is no need to project a story of a past that explains and justifies your feelings of guilt and limitation now. There is no need to project a story of a future—either a hopeful future that promises to atone for your guilt and fill your lack, or a depressing future that threatens only further guilt and loss. Your sense of guilt and limitation is understood as only the illusory reflection of your meaningless ideas of separation and guilt, of two powers, of your limitation and victimhood.

This is not to say that we should simply deny and repress our negative feelings. In order to truly heal those feelings and those perceptions, we have to acknowledge and accept them. You simply *don't add the thought* or story that something in the past or the future, something that doesn't exist now at all, is somehow causing you to feel the way you do now. When you realize that your interpretation and experience of the past and the future are *being made in the now and being projected in and from the now,* you can begin to let go of those *thoughts* about the past and the future as external powers in your life. This is forgiveness: letting go of projected stories of blame and guilt and fear. In other words, you can begin to forgive—that is, release your projected stories of—both the past and the future.

The past and the future, by definition, do not exist now and can have no effects on the now. For instance, that "terrible" person you remember from your past is not standing beside you and criticizing you now, and cannot be making you unhappy now. What exists now are only your own projected thoughts about the past and the future. When you think you are upset by some past or future event, you are really being upset by your own *thoughts* about that event.

All of this is independent of whether external time "really exists"—independent of whether something in the past "really" happened or something in the future is "really" going to occur. You are simply letting go of the *thought* that something *outside of the now* can *cause* you to feel limited or unhappy *now*. For that matter, you also let go of the thought that something *outside of the now* can *cause* you to feel good or happy *now*.

So this is not about repressing or denying painful memories or frightening anticipations. You are simply recognizing that these are *thought*s you are thinking in the now. And you can always choose to think a different thought. For instance, you might choose to remember a happier memory—after all, of the millions of memories that are available to you, why dwell on the negative ones? Or you might choose to "re-write" a painful memory. From the perspective of a separative way of thinking, this would be dishonest, because it believes that the past injury or abuse really happened and really scarred you then (and so you continue to be scarred now in every moment). But from the perspective of one power, any experience—including any memory—of victimization is always just a projection. Even if (in your remembered story now) you were so young at the time that you had no choice about whether to feel victimized, you do have that choice now. Perhaps, for instance, you have a memory of—i.e., you are currently telling yourself the story of—an unloving parent and the anguish of feeling that you were never good enough. But now the more mature you can see that you (as a be-ing of love) were always good enough and that your parent's unkindness really had nothing to do with you at all. It was simply a matter of their own fear and ignorance. But most importantly, you can choose *now* not to victimize yourself with stories of victimization and inadequacy—regardless of whether those are stories of the past or the present or the future.

The only thing that determines your happiness and peace now is your own awareness of the eternal presence of love. That awareness does not involve denying or repressing the past or the future. It is rather a matter of shifting your thoughts and focus of attention *now* and allowing yourself to be aware of the truth of love *now*. The *eternal* truth of love has nothing to do with our stories about the past and the future.

From the perspective of creative mind, you never "have to" think fearful or upsetting thoughts. There is no reality outside your mind now that can compel you to be unhappy. But only when you are free of the *belief* that something outside you and beyond your control can "make" your life limited and unhappy now, are you free to look for and discover whatever limiting thoughts you may be thinking now. And then you are free to change those thoughts and to shift your attention to something happier and more positive. In other words, you are free to consciously and deliberately live your life as *creative* mind.

The Now of Eternal Creating

From the perspective of one power and creative mind, perception is understood as an expression of your creative mind co-creating with source, the co-creative manifestation of ever-expanding source joyfully and lovingly evolving toward ever more joy and love. This now is not a moment of time, nor does this creating take place in time.

It is important to keep in mind that this account—and for that matter, this whole book—is just another possible story about experience. It does not pretend to be the final truth. Our question is whether this story can improve the quality of our lives, and allow us to experience more peace and happiness.

Earlier I said that your interpretation of what you are experiencing—of what is already under way—necessarily includes elements about the "is" and the "already" and the "under way." For the one-power perspective, however, these elements are not understood as moments in time, but as rather internal dimensions of the now of eternal creating.

The "*is*" part of your story is the part that describes your current perception. From the perspective of one power and creative mind, it describes your current awareness in terms of what you have already created and what is already manifesting in your mind.

The "*already*" part of your story is the part that explains how this current creative manifestation has come to be. From the perspective of creative mind, what you now are creatively experiencing—i.e., how source is now manifesting within your awareness—depends on what thoughts you are already thinking now. These already-being-thought thoughts are either opening or restricting the ability of your awareness to clearly manifest source. The quality of that experience is a reflection of your mind's current level of openness to feel perfect love and peace and joy now. And you know what kinds of thoughts you are *already* thinking in the now by what you are feeling now. The feelings you are feeling *now* imply the presence (in the now) of *already*-being-thought thoughts.

But it is important to note that this "already" does not refer to some particular previous moment of time. Insofar as perception is already interpreted experience, there is always an element of already-interpreted-ness inherent in perception. This can be understood as simply part of the now of perception. You do not need to add a story about previous moments in time that are "behind" you. The now of perception has an *intrinsic* dimension of already-ness in its very nature.

Understood in this way, the dimension of already-ness—which exists in your experience as your feelings—offers you an opportunity. If you are currently realizing the happy effects of already thinking allowing-thoughts, you can choose to continue to think more of those kinds of thoughts. If you are currently realizing the unhappy effects of unhappy thoughts, you can choose to think different and happier thoughts. This shift may involve identifying the restrictive thoughts you are already thinking, so that you can deliberately change them. Or it may simply be a matter of choosing to think happier and more loving thoughts that are more allowing. Either way, your primary focus is on what you are creat-ing and becom-ing *now*, rather than on what you have already created.

The "*under way*" part of your story is the part that tells where this now is headed. From the perspective of creative mind, the "under-way-ness" is no longer fearfully understood in terms of future events that are going to happen "to" you. Instead, you think of it in terms of the promise of your creativity—the ever-evolving manifestation of ever-expanding love and joy. When you understand it in this way—and you do this in the eternal now—you experience an on-going sense of gratitude, excitement and hopeful anticipation.

Two Ways of Thinking about Causality

Your story of your experience implicitly includes your story of causality, your story of how things come to be what they are. Your understanding of causality will determine what you think you need to do to change your experience.

When you are perfectly happy, there is no reason for you to do anything at all. More precisely, there is no reason for you to do anything different from what you are already doing. You simply continue to allow your awareness to fully and clearly manifest the creative power for ever-expanding well-being as the feelings and experiences of ever-expanding well-being—as happiness evolving into ever-deeper happiness.

But when you are unhappy or unpeaceful for any reason—either you simply feel unhappy, or you are having experiences that you do not like—then you want to know how to respond in a way that will improve the quality of your feelings and experiences. And your understanding of causality will determine what you do or don't do. It will determine what you can even imagine is possible.

If you choose to understand time as an external reality, you will think of causality as a linear sequence of external events. From that perspective, the past moments cause or condition the present moment and the future moments. What has happened in your past determines, at least in large part, what you are now, how you feel now, and what is possible for you now. For instance, your past can cause you to feel guilt or regret or anger now, and can leave you psychologically and emotionally scarred. And you have no control over the past now, since it has already happened.

In this way of understanding time, the past also determines, at least in large part, the future. We say that "events have already been set in motion," indicating that there is a certain inevitability to what will happen. Since the past is external to us and is out of our control, the future that follows from this past is also out of our control, at least to some degree. And the future that will necessarily follow from that past can weigh on our minds and cause us to feel fear or anxiety or depression now.

But from the perspective of one power and creative mind, causality is understood very differently. The principle of one power is the choice to believe that there is only one power, only one cause. That cause is source or love. In this context, *to cause means to create*—that is the only real meaning of causality. Source causes or creates by extending itself. And since source is the *only* cause, that means only what is of love is real. Love is the only real content of any experience, regardless of the form of the experience. The degree of your awareness of this content depends on the openness or closed-off-ness of your own mind.

The cause of this eternal creation—i.e., source or one power—is not a thing or event in time To say that this creation is eternal means that it is not a temporal process and does not take place in time. The time that we experience is simply a feature of our own understanding, a feature of the story we tell ourselves about this eternal creation. In our story, we talk about a "cause giving rise to an effect," as if an earlier event gave rise over time to a later event. That's how we tell a story: we explain and make sense of things in terms of distinct concepts strung together in linear sentences.

But from the perspective of one power, the creating is eternal—an eternal extending forth of love in the form of awareness of ever-expanding well-being. But even though we can have an inner sense of what this means, our attempts to put it into words are awkward and paradoxical. The structure of language is simply not well-suited for this: concepts are inherently dualistic and sentences are inherently linear. At best, we can point ourselves toward that inner knowing by using metaphors and analogies. As Zen Buddhism says, fingers pointing at the moon.

The Analogy of the Dream

Creation—or creating—is eternal. This means that everything you experience—including your experiences of yourself, your body, other bodies, of the world, space and time—are being eternally created in the eternal now. "Everything you experience" means both the eternal unchanging content of ever-expanding love, as well as the various ever-changing forms of experience contributed by your thoughts—thoughts which either reveal and express the content of love, or conceal and distort it.

One way that can be helpful in understanding the idea of "eternal" is to think about a dream. A whole dream can take place in a very short period of "objective" time, even in an instant. And yet that dream can include an entire story—can include memories of a past, a whole sequence of present events, and anticipations about a future. When we awaken and recall the dream, we remember—i.e., we re-member our dream experience as—a long period of time full of one event after the other. And yet this entire experience was created all at once, and existed only an instant.

Similarly, right now I seem to be in the midst of a whole sequence of events. I woke up, I exercised, I showered, I had breakfast, I sat down with a cup of coffee and started typing this section of the book on my laptop. And I can remember everything that I did yesterday and last month and last year. I remember a whole rich history starting with my childhood. And I remember—at least indirectly—a whole history that occurred before I was even born, a history that ultimately goes back to the very origin of the universe. And I am looking toward a future—later this afternoon when I go to work at our chiropractic office, tonight when I get to relax and enjoy an evening with my wife, tomorrow when I plan to put the finishing touches on my blogsite *(www.TheHappyMindBook .com)*, two weeks from now when we will celebrate Thanksgiving with our children and grandchildren, and on and on. A rich and wonderful life, full of remembered and anticipated experiences as well as an on-going drama of current experiences.

And yet I know—based on my experiences with dreams that have seemed equally real at the time I was dreaming them— that all of this long and full life I am in the midst of living and experiencing now could be an instantaneous creation of my mind. Taking it one step further, my mind could be eternally in the midst of an instantaneous creation of the story and the experience of an entire life. Taking it even further, source could be eternally in the midst of the instantaneous creation of my mind co-creating its experience of an entire life.

The purpose of this analogy is not to play an idle mind-game, but rather to try to find some reference point in our everyday experience that will help us to have a sense of what "eternal" means. In this context, the main point is that the cause—the one and only cause of everything—is not in time, nor does the "process" of causality or creation take place in time. Moreover, since this one cause is the *infinite eternal* creative power for ever-expanding well-being, it is not limited by any of its manifestations. In other words, the cause is not limited by its effects. In terms of our actual experience, this means that the creative power of source is not limited by any events in space and time—i.e., by any events our minds interpret and experience as being in space and time. We discussed this in chapter three in the section on "the now of infinite possibility."

From the perspective of one power and creative mind, the belief that one event in time causes another would be analogous to our belief that one event in a dream causes another event in the dream. Once we have awakened, however, we realize that one dream event does not cause another. We realize that *all* of the events and experiences in the dream were ultimately caused by the dreaming consciousness. For that matter, even my dreamed character's understanding of how one event causes another—his understanding of the dream world's laws of physics—even that understanding itself is created by the dreaming consciousness. For instance in some dreams, holding onto a certain object may allow you to fly. And in such a dream, this is not considered extraordinary, but simply an expression of the natural laws of that dream world.

It is important to note that when I say that all of the events in your dream were caused by the dreaming consciousness, I do not mean that they were caused or created by the dreamed "you" with its dreamed mind and body. The dreaming consciousness is at a different level from the dreamed character. Likewise, source and its extension (i.e., creative mind, pure creative awareness) are at a different level from the experience of being "a separate individual consciousness encased in a body in space and time." That whole experience of a separate consciousness in space and time is only the reflection of one possible story creative mind can tell itself. We discussed this earlier in chapter two when we made the distinction between awareness and the objects of awareness.

Healing Possibilities

The choice to believe that there is a reality external to your awareness—a reality of events in space and time that cause one another—that choice is simply one possible way of thinking, one possible story you can tell yourself. And that interpretation will define the kind and quality of experience you can be aware of.

If you think that your perceptions and your feelings are caused by an external reality, you will understand your current possibilities for experiencing healing and well-being to be, at least to some extent, determined and limited by past events. That way of understanding would effectively limit the openness of your awareness and restrict what possibilities you could experience or even imagine.

But if you believe that there is only one power, and that power is the infinite eternal creative power for well-being, then you will believe that there is no limit to the healing and well-being you can experience in any moment or in any situation, except for the limits you impose on your own awareness by thinking limiting, restricting thoughts. You will realize that your stories—including your stories of the past and the present and the future—are simply your stories, and not objective realities that victimize you and limit your happiness. This does not mean that you become foolhardy and irresponsible. Indeed the point here is to be completely responsible for your stories, rather than pretend to yourself they are simply happening "to" you.

Nothing in the past—which exists now only as your story of the past—has taken anything away from your potential to co-create your experience of well-being now. Nothing in the future can either take anything away from it or, for that matter, add anything to it. Now is always the moment of infinite possibility—the infinite potential of source energy to manifest as well-being. Your expression of this infinite potential for well-being can be limited only by your own thoughts.

To choose to believe the one-power way of thinking is to deliberately and proactively keep your mind open to unlimited possibilities of healing and well-being, including possibilities you may not be able to even conceive or imagine now. This belief implies an element of trust and surrender to something greater or higher than your own limited intellect with its limited ideas—a trust in a power or cause of infinite love and good will. This "higher" power is not understood as something separate from you, but as the very cause and truth of you and everything else. It is the cause and truth of your awareness of the unfolding drama of experiences of "yourself" and "others." "Higher" does not mean higher than yourself, but rather higher and deeper and more comprehensive than your current limited *idea* of yourself.

From the perspective of creative mind, the thought of time as a linear causal sequence of separate moments is ultimately based on the denial of mind's creativity. When you use time to project the blame for your unhappiness, you make yourself into a victim. You hide your own creative power, and you tell yourself that you *have to* be unhappy and limited now *because* of past and future events.

Ultimately, both the separation way of thinking about causality and the eternal-creative way are just possible stories we can tell ourselves to make sense of our lives. The issue here is not which story is "right" and which one is "wrong." That would imply some separate objective reality we could be "right" or "wrong" about. The real question here is "Which way of thinking will best serve you and your world?" For me, the advantage of the one-power, eternal-creation way of thinking is that it allows us to discover our full range of possibilities for well-being and happiness.

Forgiveness as Freedom from Time

Earlier we discussed the idea that "forgiveness is freedom." We saw how forgiveness could free us from the self-made mental prison of guilt and blame, and free us for love and joy. Now, in light of our current discussion of time and causality, we can see that forgiveness offers an even greater freedom. Every time you condemn another for something he has done to you, you are implicitly affirming that his past actions have made him guilty now and have made you a victim. Or if you are blaming yourself for something you did in the past, you are implicitly affirming that you are guilty and someone else is a victim. Forgiveness—simply letting go of your story of blame and guilt and victimhood—releases you from your *idea* of yourself as guilty or victimized and frees you to take over your identity as creative mind. And it offers or extends that same freedom to the other. You offer either imprisonment or freedom to both of you together.

At a more general level, to condemn someone for something is to implicitly affirm that the present is determined by the past—for instance, that the love or joy someone is capable of or deserves now is limited by what he has done in the past. Every judgment and grievance is an implicit affirmation of linear external time and linear causality—it is an implicit affirmation that your mind and your experience are determined and limited, at least to some extent, by the linear causal laws of worldly bodies. In effect, you are affirming that you are at the mercy of your body and its physical causal laws. No matter how many times you may repeat the affirmation, "now is a moment of infinite possibility," every time you hold a grievance about yourself or another you are affirming limited possibility and victimhood. That real-life belief about your own or another's guilt, often accompanied with strong emotions of shame or self-righteous anger, will effectively cancel out your theoretical affirmations of infinite possibility and creativity.

In the deepest sense, forgiveness is freedom because it frees you from the belief that you and others are somehow victims of time, victims of a material world with its own impersonal causal laws. And this has nothing to do with what you or another "really" said or did in the past—i.e., in your remembered story of the past. The point is that the now—the eternal now— is not determined by or beholden to the past, regardless of what that past is.

You cannot experience the full scope of the miraculous healing potential of the eternal now as long as you believe yourself to be defined and determined by a now-moment of linear time. You cannot experience or offer true healing as long as you hold a grudge or judgment against anyone or anything. You cannot be free of the laws of sickness and injury determining your physical well-being; you cannot be free of the laws of economic forces determining your material abundance; you cannot be free of the laws of vengeance determining your peace of mind. Forgiveness, and only forgiveness, offers you that freedom—freedom to experience the full infinite creative potential of source, which is the truth of the eternal now.

For some, this will seem to be a wildly exaggerated claim— freedom from the laws of physics, from the laws of biology, from the laws of medicine, from the laws of economics. Is complete freedom possible? I really don't know. My own life experience still seems determined, at least in large part, by those laws. But I do find that the more I forgive and the more I sink into the belief in one power and the other principles, the more I experience what I called "miracles" in chapter four above. In the example

I shared there, I was using the prayer "Let love's will become manifest in our awareness." Forgiveness is implicit in this prayer, a necessary prerequisite of extending this prayer to others. This prayer expresses the intention that love's will of perfect peace and joy become fully manifest in awareness. This means letting go of every *thought* that I or the other cannot, or does not deserve to, experience perfect well-being now.

These miracles are sometimes in the form of amazing coincidences, such as receiving resources or support from an unexpected place at just the right time. Sometimes they are in the form of discontinuities in the causal sequence of my experiences, such as suddenly becoming well or having a pain disappear—not slowly over time according to the "normal course of events," but the instantaneous disappearance of pain or sickness. These things don't happen every time. But I believe the inconsistency is only a reflection of the inconsistency of my own beliefs. I don't yet know if it's possible to be completely free of worldly laws, at least as long as I'm in the midst of worldly experience. But I do find that the more I truly forgive, the more I refuse to remain angry or judgmental for any reason, the freer I seem to be from the so-called "laws" of sickness and lack, the so-called "laws" of un-well-being. Will this work for you in your own life? You can discover the answer to this only by actually trying it.

Realizing Love's Will

Source's creative impulse or thrust toward ever-expanding well-being can be thought of as the "will" of love. In your own awareness, that creative impulse exists as a possibility, as the ever-present potential to experience joy and well-being. It is your thoughts that determine the openness of your mind to fully realize the creative possibility of love, to fully realize and complete love's will.

Realizing love's will is the deepest and most authentic possibility of your being. *In your truth, you **are** the realizing of love's will.* More precisely, you are the *possibility* of realizing love's will. Your choice of your thoughts and your focus of attention determine the degree to which you realize this possibility, the degree to which your life experience realizes love's will. The ultimate purpose of your life, the way you realize your own truth, *is* by realizing love's will in the form of feelings and experiences of love, joy and well-being.

Love's will is for the perfect well-being of everyone (including yourself). Thus, love's will *is* your will and everyone else's will. Your realization of love's will can never be in conflict with another's realization of love's will. The *only* things that determine the realization of love's will in your life are your own thoughts and focus of attention. Your experiences of the world and others are the manifestations of love's will in your awareness, as defined and limited by your thoughts. Those manifestations, however, cannot limit your mind's ability to fully and clearly realize love's will—cannot limit your mind's ability to extend love and to experience joy and well-being.

In perception consciousness, self-awareness exists as a relationship between a "you" character and something or someone else. In this kind of consciousness, love's will exists simultaneously as the love and happiness that you extend or give *to* others and the love and happiness that you receive or experience *from* others. Your giving of love and your receiving of love are two aspects of the *same* process of the realizing of love's will. To block or restrict one aspect of that process *is* to block or restrict the other. In simpler terms, you receive what you give, since your receiving is but a reflection of your giving.

The loving thoughts you extend to others, sincerely desiring them to experience ever-expanding well-being, *are* the thoughts that *allow* your own awareness to experience ever-expanding well-being. This is why your forgiveness and appreciation of others, *regardless* of whether your ego thinks they deserve it or not, are essential to your own experience of happiness and well-being.

Moreover, your forgiveness and appreciation of others help them to let go of their own restricting thoughts of guilt and fear. In other words, the forgiving, appreciative, loving thoughts that allow you to realize love's will in your own experience also help to enable others to realize it in their experience.

Love's will *is* for the perfect well-being of *everyone*. It is only by self-awarely participating in love's will—self-awarely extending unconditional love and well-being to *everyone*—that you actively create your own receptivity to experience love and happiness.

Choosing Happiness NOW

For creative mind, life *is* creative, dynamic and ever-expanding. *The true joy of life is the joy of the creating itself*—the journey of co-creatively allowing love's will of happiness and love to manifest in your own and everyone else's awareness. You can also, of course, thoroughly enjoy what is already being manifested. But self-aware creative mind thinks of what is already being manifested as simply the current expression of its on-going creative process rather than as some external reality. It understands manifestation as the effect of its happiness, and not the cause.

Now *is* the moment of co-creating, and now is the only time you can self-awarely live your creative truth. Now *is* the moment of choice—choosing either to extend allowing thoughts of love, or to project restricting thoughts of guilt and fear. And you know which kinds of thoughts you are thinking by how you feel. If you are feeling happy now, you are already in the midst of extending happy and loving thoughts. If you are feeling unhappy now, you are already in the midst of projecting unhappy and unloving thoughts.

Happiness *is* the emotional reflection of self-awarely living your creative truth, self-awarely allowing love's will to manifest itself in your awareness. You can *be* self-aware only in the now. Now *is* the moment of happiness, and happiness *is* living the truth of the now.

Only when you lose sight of the truth of now do you feel unhappy. And that unhappiness is another moment of choice for you. You can choose to look in hopeless despair to some story of an irrevocable past of guilt and loss. Or you can choose to look to some story of the future and tell yourself that you can be happy only later, *only after* you have overcome the wounds of a difficult past, *only after* you have somehow paid for your past "sins" and mistakes, *only after* you have triumphed over adverse circumstances, *only after* you know more and have accomplished more, *only after* you have gotten more fame or money or power or better relationships.

Or, you can simply choose to think a happier, more loving thought *now*. You can choose to shift your thinking and your focus of attention, in the trust that when you allow your own awareness to be more open to realizing love's will, the manifestation of ever-expanding well-being is the inevitable result.

Your happier thought could be a thought about the past or the present or the future. Or it could be a happier thought about one power and the eternal now of creating. The particular form of the thought is irrelevant. What matters is whether the thought allows you to be aware of the presence of love now.

In choosing happiness now, you are choosing to be in the midst of already thinking a happy thought. And you are choosing to be under way toward ever-expanding love and happiness. So in this sense, choosing happiness now for yourself *is* choosing happiness "for all time."

Remember that any unhappiness that you are feeling, you are feeling *now*, because now is the only time you can feel anything at all. And that unhappiness is being caused by some restricting thought that you are thinking now, because now is the only time you can actually think anything at all. Even if the unhappiness you are feeling now is associated with a memory of some past event, you are actually remembering that event and feeling that unhappiness *now*. Likewise, if the unhappiness you are feeling now is associated with the anticipation of some future event, you are anticipating that event and feeling that unhappiness *now*. So regardless of what time you associate your unhappiness with, the most appropriate response is to once again choose happiness *now*.

In your truth, you *are* a realizing of love's will. The purpose and goal of your life is to clearly and fully manifest love's will, both in extending forth loving and happy thoughts, and in manifesting and experiencing happy experiences. This goal is not a static destination, but rather an eternal process of becoming, an eternal process of co-creating, an eternal process of realizing ever-expanding well-being. And your role in realizing love's will—which is, in truth, your own will—is to continually choose and re-choose whatever thought or focus of attention brings more love and joy to your awareness now.

When you deliberately choose to shift your focus of attention to something that feels better, what you are really doing is finding that place in your mind in which you are aware of the presence of love. And then you are choosing a thought that somehow keeps you more open to that awareness. When you choose to think a happier thought, your happiness is not caused by that particular thought. Your happiness is simply the emotional reflection of your awareness of the eternal presence of love, your awareness of your own truth and essence.

Happiness is the promise and the goal of life. When you choose love and happiness in each moment of your life, you live happily. When you live happily, your life experiences reflect and manifest love and joy, and you inspire others. Choosing and re-choosing love and happiness now *is* how you fully and self-awarely realize your truth, and fulfill your purpose.

Now is the eternal moment of choice, the moment in which you can choose again. *Now is the eternal opportunity to choose love.* It makes no difference to creative mind what you have chosen before. If you find yourself already in the midst of feelings and experiences that tell you that you are already thinking restricting thoughts, then just choose again now. Re-choose now to be who you truly are. Re-choose now to shift your attention to the happiest thoughts you are capable of at this moment. Re-choose now to extend love. Re-choose now to think thoughts that allow love's will to manifest in your life. Re-choose now to realize love's will in your life.

Practicing the Principle of Choosing Happiness *Now*

In your experience, the past and the future exist only as your *thoughts* of the past and the future *now.* How do your current thoughts of the past and the future affect how you feel now? If your thoughts of the past or the future are making you unpeaceful or unhappy now, how could you change those thoughts? How do you *want* to feel now? What kinds of thoughts about the past and future would support that way of feeling?

As you find yourself under way toward a future of ever-expanding well-being and happiness, focus your attention on the joy of the creative process itself. This is not a matter of denying your goals. But you don't have to put off your happiness until you've reached the "destination" of your current creative journey. Simply appreciate and enjoy the creative process itself—the joy of being the loving creative mind that creates desires and then creatively translates those desires into experience. Enjoy being eternally under way toward ever-expanding love and goodness.

Monitor how you feel moment to moment. When you feel good, you are thinking a downstream or allowing thought. When you feel bad, you are thinking an upstream or restricting thought.

When you find yourself feeling unhappy, remind yourself that everything you want is downstream. In that moment, shift your attention to a happier thought—to the happiest thought you are capable of thinking at that time. Notice any resistance in yourself to making this shift, any reasons or excuses you give yourself for continuing to think an unhappy thought.

In every moment, ask yourself, "How could I be happier now?" And remember, the answer is always a shift in your own awareness.

CONCLUSION

Happiness always exists in the now. Happiness is how you feel in the now when you are self-awarely living your truth. In the same way that awakening from a dream is a possibility that is available in every moment of the dream, so too is happiness a possibility that is inherent in every moment of life. It is not something that you have to win or achieve in the future when you have done more or accumulated more or know more. Nor is it something that you will gain only after you have mastered these seven principles for happiness. It is your truth now, and every moment is an opportunity to allow it to shine forth in your awareness. And when it shines forth in your awareness, it brings more light into everyone's awareness.

In the simplest terms, the way to be happy and to have a happy life is simply to choose to be happy now. The way to co-create a happy life is to happily co-create in every now. When you are feeling happy, then this simple advice makes perfect sense. You don't need any principles or practices, you don't need any spiritual theories—you just choose to be happy.

But when your core beliefs do not allow your mind to be perfectly happy, you will find yourself feeling unhappy, at least sometimes and to some degree. Because this process is subconscious, you are unaware of the role your core beliefs are playing. When you are unhappy, your mind makes reasons and explanations for your unhappiness and projectively makes unhappy experiences to reinforce your unhappiness. From within that kind of life experience, it can seem difficult or impossible to simply choose to be happy, for that choice flies in the face of everything you perceive and believe. To simply choose to be happy seems to be naive, foolish and unrealistic at best, and perhaps even insane, dangerous or morally irresponsible. It is then that you need some other way of thinking about your life.

These seven principles for happiness offer one possible way to think about and relate to yourself and the world—a way that can allow you to experience more happiness in your life and to more fully realize your deepest desires.

The principle of one power is the foundation for the very possibility of perfect happiness. Any belief in more than one power will always introduce conflict and fear into your experience.

The principle of creative mind reminds you that you are a creative extension of source, and that *your* experience *is* the reflection of *your* thoughts. You are not a victim of hostile forces. In choosing your thoughts, you are choosing the quality or tone of your awareness and thus the degree of well-being and happiness you can experience.

The principle of allowing happiness is an extension of the principle of one power. It reminds us that moving toward greater happiness is not a struggle against forces of unhappiness. It is rather a matter of ceasing to think the kinds of thoughts that hide our natural happiness, and choosing to think instead thoughts that *allow* our minds to fully manifest the creative potential for happiness and well-being that is our very truth.

The principle of joyful manifestation clarifies how your happiness-based desires give form to the infinite creative power for well-being in your own life experience. Your role in the process of manifestation is to think allowing thoughts. Happy thoughts are creatively reflected as joyful manifestations.

The principle of forgiveness is freedom explains how forgiveness is really the undoing of your unconscious self-deception. Your extension of forgiveness, which includes your extension of innocence and invulnerability, undoes and heals the misperceptions caused by your projection of separation and guilt and victimhood. It frees you from the negative judgmental thoughts about yourself and the world that restrict your mind's ability to experience happiness and well-being.

The principle of love is being yourself reminds you that the kinds of thoughts that allow you to experience happiness and well-being are loving thoughts. You *are* an expression of love. Self-awarely being yourself—deliberately extending forth unconditional love to everyone, including yourself—*is* being happy. Being loving *is* being happy, and being happy *is* being loving.

The principle of choosing happiness *now* explores a new way to understand now as an eternal moment of creation. The one cause of your awareness and experience expresses itself as the eternal creating of feelings and experiences of love and joy and well-being. Ultimately, your ideas and experiences of linear time and worldly causality exist in your awareness as the result of projecting your mistaken ideas of separation and victimhood. From the perspective of the now of eternal creation, every moment *is* the opportunity to choose love—to choose love for *all* time. The moment-to-moment choosing and re-choosing of love *is* self-awarely living your truth, and is reflected as a happy mind experiencing a happy life.

There is, of course, no "should" involved in any of this. There is nothing wrong in being unhappy, nor is unhappiness something to feel guilty about. You are free to be as unhappy as you wish and free to think about and focus on what you don't like. But when you choose a thought or a focus, you also choose its consequences.

Every moment of unhappiness multiplies itself. If you choose to think a thought that makes you feel unhappy, you are also choosing to manifest unhappy experiences. In every moment that you spend in judgment, guilt, fear, anger, hatred, frustration, despair or depression, not only are you making yourself unhappy in that moment, but you are also actively restricting the realization of all of your desires.

Every moment of happiness multiplies itself as well. If you choose to think a thought that makes you feel happy, you are also choosing to have happy experiences. Every moment that you spend in appreciation and love, in peace and happiness, you are actively allowing your mind to manifest the infinite abundance and benevolence of source in every area of your life experience.

It comes down to a simple choice. Do you want to feel unhappy and not realize your dreams? Or do you want to feel happy and manifest your deepest and truest desires?

When you have interpreted the world in only one way for your whole life—especially if this is the way that "everyone else" also interprets it—you tend to be unaware that it is an interpretation at all. You assume that you are merely seeing and describing "how things are." It is only when you become aware of an alternative interpretation that you can recognize, for the first time, that your own interpretation is indeed an "interpretation." And then, for the first time, you are freed to consciously *choose* an interpretation—to choose one that best serves you.

The real purpose of this book is to provide one possible alternative interpretation to the one we all tend to take for granted—an interpretation that allows you to become aware of your current interpretation, and to re-choose if you want to.

I have tried to show some of the presuppositions of the "everyday taken-for-granted" way of thinking. I have explored the implications of that way of thinking for how we feel and how we experience our lives. We have seen that this interpretation necessarily gives rise to feelings and experiences of unhappiness and un-well-being.

The seven principles for happiness offer an alternative way of thinking based on alternative fundamental ideas. And these fundamental ideas have radically different implications for how we feel, and how we experience ourselves and the world.

You have no choice whether to choose your core beliefs. You are always already in the midst of living some choice, whether consciously or subconsciously. And your choice necessarily has consequences in terms of what you can experience, how you can feel and how you can influence others in your life. Since this *is* your life, you would like to choose wisely.

The question here is will *these* principles and practices work for *you* in your own life? It is said that, "The proof of the pudding is in the eating." This means that the only way to know if the pudding is good is to actually taste it yourself. The only way to find out if these principles and practices can transform your life experience is to actually live them, in your own way following your own inner guidance.

From the perspective of these seven principles for happiness, our purpose is to allow the love that is the source of all life to manifest clearly and deeply in our lives and to extend through our lives into the lives of others. Our role in this co-creative process is to choose and re-choose love and happiness in every moment, in every now. That choice allows the loving power of life to manifest in our lives as feelings and experiences of love and happiness and well-being. Then our lives become the living realization of the creative power of love. Happiness is the promise and the goal of life, and *we* are the fulfillment of that promise.

ABOUT THE AUTHOR

D r. William Yoder has a doctorate in philosophy, and has studied Eastern and Western philosophy and religion for over forty years. His doctoral dissertation on comparative mysticism was hailed by Dr. Huston Smith: "thoroughly rewarding, instructive, and original, and it advances the philosophical treatment of mysticism." Dr. Yoder taught university philosophy courses for ten years at the University of Buffalo, Vassar College and Furman University.

He left the academic world to pursue a career in holistic healing. He and his wife earned their doctorates in chiropractic, and have practiced in their upstate New York clinic for over twenty years.

Throughout this time, he continued his active exploration of philosophy and spirituality. He studied with the Option Institute (founded by Barry Neil Kaufman), and with such teachers as

Ram Dass, Thich Nhat Hanh, Michael Harner, Gail Straub, David Gershon, and Wallace Black Elk.

He has also been a student of *A Course in Miracles* for over twenty years. During the past five years he has taught a class on the Course. These classes have been recorded and the CDs are available.

Over the past twenty years, he and his wife have given presentations and taught workshops in both the private and the corporate sectors on the topics of health and healing, human potential, self-actualization and spirituality.

Dr. Yoder has also written *Lighted Clearings for the Soul* (2004). His next book, *Lighted Clearings of Possibility* (provisional title) is due out in the spring of 2011.

For more information about Dr. Yoder's CDs, speaking engagements, workshops, and books, visit

www.TheHappyMindBook.com